Write Now!

WESTERN ENGLAND

Edited by Allison Dowse

First published in Great Britain in 2003 by
YOUNG WRITERS
Remus House,
Coltsfoot Drive,
Peterborough, PE2 9JX
Telephone (01733) 890066

All Rights Reserved

Copyright Contributors 2003

HB ISBN 1 84460 176 5
SB ISBN 1 84460 177 3

FOREWORD

This year, Young Writers proudly presents a showcase of the best short stories and creative writing from today's up-and-coming writers.

We set the challenge of writing for one of our four themes - 'Myths & Legends', 'Hold The Front Page', 'A Day In The Life Of . . .' and 'Short Stories/Fiction'. The effort and imagination expressed by each individual writer was more than impressive and made selecting entries an enjoyable, yet demanding, task.

Write Now! Western England is a collection that we feel you are sure to enjoy - featuring the very best young authors of the future. Their hard work and enthusiasm clearly shines within these pages, highlighting the achievement each piece represents.

We hope you are as pleased with the final selection as we are and that you will continue to enjoy this special collection for many years to come.

Contents

Birkenhead High School, Wirral
Siân Vickers	1
Holly Riley	2
Malvika Bhatia	3
Kirsten Lewis	4
Dimitra Petropoulou	6
Rachael Pratt	7
Rachael Lockyer	8
Sophie Ormond	9
Chloë O'Brien	10
Laura Stocks	11
Hannah Smith	12
Becky Woods	14
Alice Shead	15
Hannah Gilbert	16
Kelsey Williams	17
Kate Hughes	18

Chesterfield High School, Merseyside
Natalie Hall	19
Amanda Hall	20
Helen Gadie	21
Karen Brimage	22
Alison Dean	23
Siobhan O'Hagan	24
Alecia Marshall	26

Cloughside School, Manchester
Adam Stannard	27

Dulverton Middle & Community School, Somerset
Tanya Robins	28
Emma Sorrell	29
Emma Harris	30
Rosalie Tribe	31
Luchia Pike	32

	Paula White	33
	Rachael Dale	34
	Katie Lock	35

Grittleton House School, Wiltshire

	Joanne Clark	36
	Bonnie Renicks	37
	Sarah Halfacree	38
	Charles Hamilton	39
	Luke Williams	40
	David Watson	41
	Samuel Rogers	42
	Thomas Crosby	43
	Lucy Rivers	44
	Roslyn Jackson	45
	Chris Habgood	46
	Drew Richardson	47
	Jessica Carwardine	48
	Jodie Cleeves	49
	Laura Bailey	50
	Georgina Clark	51
	Eve Lewis	52
	Adam Longhurst	53
	Jonathon Shergold	54
	Katherine Trim	55
	Guy Pilbeam	56
	Alexander Bailey	57
	Alexandra Black	58
	Jasmine Lewis	59
	Matthew Mumford	60
	Victoria Rich	61

Hardenhuish School, Wiltshire

	Rebecca Crisp	62
	Max Cliverd	63
	Emily Tudgay	64
	Jon Day	65
	Joseph Doliczny	66

Kate Ellis	67
Chris Munden	68
Chris Lewis	69
David Brown	70
Jessica Davies	71
Dayna James	72
Chris Young	73
Hannah Jones	74
Andrea Wetton	75
Elizabeth Pullin	76
Chaz Sartain	78

Kingsdon Manor School, Somerset

Jamie Bessell	79
Ashley Mullen	80

Lockleaze School, Bristol

Sam Stephens	83

Maricourt RC High School, Liverpool

Katherine Bannon	84

Moorland School, Lancashire

Judith Clark	85

Norton Hill School, NE Somerset

Jo Cribb	88
Emma Pink	89
Samantha Austin	90
Olivia McGlone	92

Penwortham Girls' High School, North Somerset

Emma Wilding	93
Lauri Smith	94

Priory Community School, North Somerset

Amy Cabble	95
Kirsty Holburd	96

Jamie Rosser	97
Emma Douglas	98
Ali O'Brien	99
Luke Patrick	100
Caroline Quick	101
Harriet Glimstead	102
Rachel Rowlands	103
Sam Stitson	104
Kerry Knight	105
Craig Davies	106
Matthew Tucker	107
Jasmine Harrison	108
Amy Coppack	109
Jade Elizabeth Pickett	110
Ben Rogers	111
Harvie Agnew	112
Alex Knapp	113
Ben Harris	114
Charlotte Warren	115
Kirstie Keir	116
Joe Fisher	117
Oliver Hughes	118
Emma Perks	119
Dan Slade	120
Cherryanne Pullinger	121
Jessica Hooper-Gauci	122
Lawrence Rowland	123
Mark Bell	124
Mitchell Ford	125
Matthew Brown	126
Heidi Kyte	127
Lara Stenner	128
Kate Evans	129
Chloe Loader	130
Joshua Redmond	131
William Price	132
Matt Hedges	133
Martin Thomas	134

St Laurence School, Wiltshire
> Hannah Whittock 135
> Niall Allsopp 136
> Max Mulvany 137

Stonyhurst College, Lancashire
> Adam Morgan 138
> Charlotte Walsh 139
> Gregory Kelly 140
> Isabella Gee 141
> Timothy Lewis 142
> Anthony Hines 143
> Robert Plumbridge 144
> Dane Cimpoias 145
> Gregory Wood 146
> Robert Woolley 147
> Yvette Spedding 148
> Annabel Gale 149
> Anne Rawsthorn 150
> Serena Marchetta 151
> Harry Reid 152
> Victoria Robinson 153
> Eliza-Maria Warrilow 154
> Kendall Ellen Sharples 155
> James Rawstron 156
> Natalie Russell-Blackburn 157
> Ralph Parish 158
> Mwewa Kaluba 159
> Lizzie Coles 160

Wentworth High School, Manchester
> Mark Ashworth 161
> Damon Whitbread 162
> Sarah-Louise Morris 163
> Victoria Harrison 164
> Robert Grubisic 165
> Georgina Burrows 166

Kathryn Vickers	168
Sarah Morris	169
Liam Bell	170
Max Leonard	171

The Creative Writing

MY GIRL

She smoothly stepped out onto the porch, looked up at the sky and started to walk onto the pavement. The further she went down the road I began to notice how gracefully she walked. She was easily moving, like a swan upon water.

The sun shone brightly that day, making her hair glisten in the sun. It was let loose, trailing down her back and freely blowing in the gentle breeze. Sometimes it would blow across her face covering her emerald-green eyes that twinkled.

After a while she paused to look out on the horizon. She was tall but when she leaned against a long, lean tree, she seemed to look smaller, but when she carried on walking she was her normal height and her normal size.

She had a beautiful figure but had a small bone structure. Not an ounce of flab was anywhere, most women would love to have her figure. Long legs, flat stomach and beautiful skin without a single pimple. It was fair with red, rosy cheeks.

She was wearing a pair of red shorts that had a number 72 on them with a matching string strappy top. She was carrying a navy bag which also had a 72 on. On her feet she was wearing flip-flops that matched her painted toenails. Her long slender hands firmly gripped her bag. Her perfect nails were painted a fluorescent blue that reflected the sun. She had a round freckle above her lip, on the right and a beauty spot on her left shoulder. Her lips were the colour of a deep red rose and her pierced ears had a pair of diamond earrings in, sparkling in every way. She was gorgeous.

Siân Vickers (13)
Birkenhead High School, Wirral

BEWARE OF INNOCENT DRINKS

On 21st March 2003 at the Crown Courts in Liverpool, known to skaters for the surrounding open space, an incident took place at 2.15pm. A group of young teenagers, hot after skating had gone to a nearby stall to purchase bottles of Coke.

After just a mouthful, the youngest member immediately fell ill and fell to the ground. His friends skated off leaving him alone, unconscious on the floor. A passer-by raised the alarm and an ambulance arrived promptly to take the semi-conscious boy straight to Alder Hey hospital. It was diagnosed that fourteen-year-old Jay from West Kirby on the Wirral had drunk contaminated Coke which contained anti-freeze.

After four days of intensive care, Jay is now off the critical list.

The family would like to thank the passer-by, whose name is not known, for preventing a death by the swift action taken.

This is the third case reported in the Merseyside area over the past six months.

Investigations are currently under way to determine how and who had contaminated the Coke.

Holly Riley (13)
Birkenhead High School, Wirral

A Day In The Life Of An Unknown Writer

I have won the Nobel Prize for the best-selling author of inspirational stories. As I waved to the crowd, my alarm went off and I woke up at my writing desk. I had fallen asleep last night while re-writing the climax of my book, *Being Unknown.*

I got dressed, picked up my tattered bag and my hand-written book and stepped out to face another hectic day of being thrown out of offices of big publishers.

The first publisher I went to said that my story was very lengthy. The second one said it was very commendable, but they couldn't publish it. Thus I was roaming around town till dusk. As always I wasn't expecting to be recognised. I've been rejected so many times this had become a habit, but it is also very discouraging. I read the first few lines of my story again -

'It is different being unknown. But it's a different plight altogether to be an unknown author. The writer has compiled so many stories which have been appreciated locally. But after working so hard on beautiful tales, trying hard to get them to the knowledge of the world, the writer is still undiscovered. The feeling when you are not complimented for doing your best, the feeling of being unrequited and unidentified, the feeling the sun might have for giving life to us but still not being appreciated. These are the few sentiments of an undiscovered writer. These are my feelings. I am the unknown writer.'

Malvika Bhatia (13)
Birkenhead High School, Wirral

WHERE WILL IT END?

I am writing this account so that in years to come my species will know the truth. The truth being that the world we presently eat, breathe and sleep in is not our own.

We were given the greatest gifts of all, life and a home, and we ungratefully threw them away. What did we do? I hear you ask. Well, we unfortunately advanced to the era of nuclear weapons. The threat of these weapons were the cause of The Great War Of The Land. The world was split in two; the north and the south. Each region would bombard the enemy with nuclear weapons, which caused mass murder and destruction of the land. The Great War lasted over a hundred years until the air itself was fatal to breathe. Eventually both colonies abandoned this world and headed to the stars in the few space shuttles that had not been reduced to small fragments of metal.

My species travelled for many light years to the nearest hospitable planet. As it came into view, my stomach lurched; how could we be sure we wouldn't mistreat this planet as we had our own?

Our space shuttles landed smoothly on the surface of this unknown planet. People flowed out of the shuttles quicker than stampeding elephants, as it had been a long time since we had all tasted clean air. Suddenly a scream arose from the crowd and not a penny dropping could be heard as the natives of the planet moved towards the shuttle. Fortunately for us they were a peaceful species who welcomed us with open arms to share their planet. They were incredibly tolerant of our destructive behaviour but eventually they could stand us no longer. The natives did not have the power to remove us, so they removed themselves.

A treaty was signed by the leaders of my species and it was agreed that our children and our children's children would never know the shameful secret of our homeland. It was agreed that we should strive to create a peaceful society in which everyone is equal. What are we and where are we from? That is the question that must be answered. Well, we are humans and we come from the planet Earth.

Kirsten Lewis (14)
Birkenhead High School, Wirral

THE LOST CITY OF ATLANTIS

Over 11,000 years ago existed an island located in the middle of the Atlantic Ocean. It was populated by a big and powerful race. The people of this land were wealthy due to natural resources found throughout the island. This was the island of Atlantis.

Atlantis was the domain of Poseidon, who was god of the sea. When Poseidon fell in love with a mortal woman, Cleito, he created a dwelling at the top of a hill near to the middle of the island. He surrounded this hill with rings of water and land to protect her. At the top of the hill there was a temple built to honour Poseidon. This housed a giant gold statue of Poseidon riding a chariot pulled by winged horses.

Later in life, Cleito gave birth to five sets of twin boys who became the first rulers of Atlantis.

For many generations the people of Atlantis lived in peace, but soon greed and power began to corrupt them. Zeus (the god of all gods) saw the immorality of the Atlanteans and gathered all the other gods to establish a suitable punishment. Soon, in one violent surge, it was gone. The island of Atlantis and its people were swallowed by the sea.

The story or myth was told by Plato, a Greek philosopher and teacher. Many people thought he had made this up; but in the last century there has been evidence found of an ancient civilisation and traces of their island underwater in the Atlantic Ocean.

Dimitra Petropoulou (14)
Birkenhead High School, Wirral

SENEX

Senex is the king of a fictional race I have created called the Abies. He is 83 years old and looks weak and frail. He has wrinkled, oily, olive-coloured skin. He has a few wisps of silvery grey tufts of hair on his otherwise bald head. He has cold, hard eyes which are neither friendly nor welcoming. He has ink blot pupils and stony grey irises. His small, skinny, scrawny body is hunched up inside an expensive designer suit.

If you were to pass him in the street you would think nothing of this small, pitiful nobody. Subconsciously, Senex is aware of this and takes advantage of his power and position as king. Beneath his frail exterior he has a terrifying temper bubbling underneath, waiting to be let out.

To make up for his frail-looking exterior there is a strong but evil man inside. He is selfish, arrogant and hateful. He is hated by his people - even his own daughter Sarri, who just wants him to love her. He punishes enemies harshly - sometimes even with death. He is extremely stubborn and hates his enemy race - the Grinds.

Sometimes, however, when he is alone, painful memories from the past come back to haunt him and he becomes the self-pitying person he appears to be. He is a sad, lonely and melancholy man who is feared by everyone. He had forgotten how to love many years ago, leaving his old heart cold and empty.

Rachael Pratt (14)
Birkenhead High School, Wirral

CHARACTER DESCRIPTION

His flowing fountain of silvery hair cascaded around his bony, hunched shoulders. His arms were thin and wizened and ended in gnarled claw-like fingers. His face looked as though it had been chiselled away and his mouth was no more than a gash across his gaunt, lifeless face. His clothes appeared to have once been fine and grand, but they had been worn away and looking at the dinner jacket hanging off his weak, thin body, you could see the carelessly spilt drops of food he had not bothered to wash away.

He was a man that had lost hope. His body was a shell for a lifeless soul. His face was dull and expressionless. A smile never crossed his face as he went about his life, not a grin or a frown and a tear has ever once fallen down his crinkled cheek. His eyes were the only part of him that showed any form of emotion and it was obvious.

Fear; it controlled his life, it made him jump at every creak and lock every door before he went to bed. He spoke to no one and lived his life shadowed from the world outside, the world past the high walls surrounding his crumbling house with the wild and uncared for garden.

Rachael Lockyer (14)
Birkenhead High School, Wirral

DESCRIBING A CHARACTER

Mrs Harrison had a perfect home, a husband and a son called Sammy and in their opinion there was no finer boy anywhere, but in fact he was the most despicable boy in the village, who got whatever he wanted. Mrs Harrison had everything she always wanted - a beautiful home and an ideal family.

Mrs Harrison was tall and thin, with blonde wavy hair that hung loosely off her pale bony face. She had an unusually elongated neck, which came in useful as she spent most of her time craning it, spying over garden fences. Mrs Harrison didn't just spend her time prying, she also cooked a lot. Whilst her husband went to work and her son went to school, Mrs Harrison cooked! She mostly made sticky, fattening desserts for her plump son. It was surprising how thin she was considering what she cooked.

It may seem that Mrs Harrison had the perfect life but in fact she was very lonely. Nobody came to visit her as she had no friends and as she came from an adopted family who had sadly passed away, she had no family.

Whilst the neighbours spent their time ignoring Mrs Harrison because she was interfering, or maybe just because they were jealous of her perfect life, they never took the time to get to know her. She may have seemed meddlesome and stuck-up and she may have looked like an adult, but really she had the heart of a sad, lonely child.

Sophie Ormond (14)
Birkenhead High School, Wirral

DESCRIPTION OF A CHARACTER

Peter Rabbit is a brown-haired, cheeky and daring little baby bunny. He is a burrowing animal, about as big as a cat, with soft fur, a short fluffy tail, long hind legs and long ears. He has many, many siblings who are known as the Flopsy Bunnies. But he is by far the most mischievous and disobedient out of them all!

Peter Rabbit is known by many children as the rabbit who wears the blue woolly cardigan with the two blue buttons on it. His shoes are black and slipper-like and Peter Rabbit is famous for always losing one of them, especially in Mr McGregor's vegetable patch. This is because Peter Rabbit is always sneaking into Mr McGregor's garden, to eat his cabbages and lettuces, after his mother specifically tells him not to, before his tea.

Mr McGregor is always trying to catch Peter Rabbit and turn him into rabbit pie. This is because he continually returns to the garden and Mr McGregor is a mean, nasty old man.

The main story is Peter Rabbit going into the garden and only escaping by the skin of his teeth before Mr McGregor catches him.

Chloë O'Brien (14)
Birkenhead High School, Wirral

A Day In The Life Of A Cloud

When I awoke this morning, I started off as cold water.

The temperature started to get a little warmer, I began to feel queasy; I was being pumped into a tube. I no longer felt cold and had stopped looking like water, I had changed into a soft, fluffy cloud.

I struggled, trying to escape from the tube; finally I succeeded.

There was a strange feeling above me; it felt as though someone was pushing me in the wrong direction. I realised that the wind was pushing me.

I floated through the air, slowly and carefully, until I knew what I was doing. There were voices in the distance saying, 'That cloud is as white as snow.' I was so proud of myself.

Oh no! There was suddenly a gust of wind and it sent me flying higher into the sky. I was frightened. The higher I went, the hotter I got. I looked up to see what was happening and there in front of me was a bright light. I named it the sun.

I could not believe that I had reached the sun before all of my friends. Oh, they would be jealous.

Just down below, I heard grumbling from the people, I was blocking their sunlight and they were angry. I moved slowly and began to tease them, swaying backwards and forwards.

Whilst I moved, I began to melt. This meant I was turning back into water once again.

Laura Stocks (13)
Birkenhead High School, Wirral

TROUBLE

'No.'
'Why?'
'Just no.'
'Come on, it won't hurt you.'
'It will.'
'How?'
'It just will, OK?'
'OK, OK, but you lose out.'
'I can live with it.'

It had been two years since Aaron had refused to join the gang that ruled by terror - turning down the invitation of a friend (acting on the gang's instructions) to accompany him on a *trip*, ie shoplifting.

He had since moved schools and was happily ensconced in his fresh surroundings, without the constant pressure of the Watley lot. He'd found new mates, worked as he'd never known he could; he'd even got himself a girl. The Watley gang had virtually faded from his mind altogether. But suddenly, one beautiful April morning, that all changed and his new world was turned upside down.

It began no different to any other. He was walking to school - it was close enough and he enjoyed the spring feeling all around him. Jen lived opposite the park and Tom a bit further on. He'd meet them at their front gates.

This morning Jen wasn't there, so he strode up the gravel path and tapped gently. A few minutes passed, a jeering laugh broke through the morning stillness. It was familiar. Aaron willed it to be his imagination, prayed he was dreaming or delirious or *something* - just that it was not who he thought it was.
'Hey scumbag, gone deaf or summat?' The call came, accompanied by shouts of laughter. With a sinking feeling in the pit of his stomach, Aaron turned. It *was* who he thought it was.

The door opened behind him.

'Aaron . . . sorry . . . . clock's wrong . . . Joseph . . . Aaron, what's wrong?'

'Nothing Jen, nothing at all. Come on, we'll be late.'

They walked down the drive, Aaron studiously, keeping his eyes fixed on the road ahead.

'Hey, hey lads! D' y' 'ear 'im? *Come on we'll be late,'* Jay jumped down from his seat in an ash and imitated Aaron in an exaggerated voice. 'Look at 'im walking down the street, pretty girl on 'is arm, thinkin' 'e's as good as any of us. Needs teachin' a lesson don't 'e lads?'

A chorus of *ayes* greeted this announcement as they moved on Aaron and Jen. They turned to leave but mocking faces grinned at them, every which way.

Aaron stepped in front of Jen. 'What do you want, Jay.' It wasn't a question.

'What do we want boys?' Jay laughed. It wasn't a pleasant laugh. Aaron knew he was in trouble. The Watley lads were back.

Hannah Smith (13)
Birkenhead High School, Wirral

THE DAY EVERYTHING CHANGED

One morning I woke up, had a wash, got dressed and went downstairs for breakfast. Mum and Alan were sitting at the table with big smiling faces. I thought they had just won the lottery or something. Mum told me to sit down because she thought what they were going to say would come as a bit of a shock. So I sat down.
My mum said, 'Becky, Alan and I, well, we're getting married.'
I sat there for a moment, opening and closing my mouth. My mum said I looked like a goldfish! I stood up and said, very slowly, 'Congratulations,' and walked out of the room. I was totally spellbound. I couldn't believe what I'd just heard!

Mum told me that everything was booked and that she was going to get married in the winter (she was only getting married in the winter so that they could go somewhere hot on their honeymoon). But that wasn't the worst, them getting married, it was the bridesmaid's dress. It was horrible! It was pink with lots of frills and bows. I refused to wear it, but, after a bit of persuasion, my mum finally convinced me to.

It was the big day. My mum's dress was gorgeous. It was as white as a swan and it was really pretty. The whole ceremony went really well. We then went to the registry office to have some photographs taken. Then we went to a restaurant for something to eat. The food was outstanding, I've never tasted anything like it in my life!

Alan then proposed a toast. Him and my mum had bought presents for everyone, so next they handed all the presents out. I got a nine-carat gold necklace. It shone like the sun. Then Alan said all the thank yous and he and my mum left in a limousine for their dream honeymoon in Hawaii.

A few weeks later I woke up, had a wash, got dressed and went downstairs for breakfast. Alan was there.

It's very strange to see Alan every morning and know that he is my stepdad.

Becky Woods (13)
Birkenhead High School, Wirral

A Day In The Life Of A Penny

It's early morning and here I am lying in a cash till. It's very dark and cold; the shop hasn't opened for business yet. According to the pounds this is a newsagent's.

By ten-thirty I have my first job, a little old lady comes to buy the morning paper, I am her change. I get shoved into a black leather purse that smells of tobacco. For the next half hour I am jostled around in her purse until I am unceremoniously thrown into a beggar's hat on the street.

It isn't the nicest of places; there is a load of tough, big bully two pences boasting about how they are worth two of me.

I lay there till late afternoon, ignoring the other coins, until the beggar packs up for the day. All the other coins are put into his pocket, except me. I am the favourite, he says, I am his lucky penny; he would keep me forever. Little did he know I would be leaving him shortly.

The beggar puts me in the back pocket of his jeans. Unfortunately there is a hole in it, but he does not know this. As he reaches the bottom of the street I slip out of the small hole in the pocket.

I fall onto the rain-splattered ground. I am soaked right through to the core and am feeling very miserable.

After what seems like hours my rescuer comes, a policeman on his beat. His warm, firm hands pick me up and carefully place me in his palm. He then closes his fist. My bed for the night.

Alice Shead (13)
Birkenhead High School, Wirral

THURSDAY

No going back this time, you have nowhere to run and nowhere to hide. Accept the straightness of your horizon and the block that ends it.

I woke with a start and quickly noted down everything that I had been told in the dream. You see as the months have gone by I have learned to trust these dreams as almost all of them have come true in the last few weeks. The past few have left me riddles that I have had to find out. I know the end will come soon.

The clues that I have are pointing to one day - Friday. I don't know how to figure out what's going to happen next when I want to just like that, but I know that it, thing, or whatever you want to call it has been following me for some time now, I can feel it . . .

Thursday night - my dream . . .

So you know that I'm hinting and playing with you, but you're not quite sure what to think yet are you . . . ?

I don't know who to turn to, I'm locked away in a room with my fear.

Friday, daytime, the corridor at the end of school.

I know the answer to the Thursday dream - the corridor that I'm in it's, it's, it's *here*.

Hannah Gilbert (13)
Birkenhead High School, Wirral

A Day In The Life Of My Dog

My name is Lucy. Allow me to give you the four-one-one on my daily twenty-four hours.

I usually sleep in till about nine-thirty and wake up with a loud yawn and a prolonged stretch. Breakfast is due at around ten to ten-thirty and I have dried cereal, known as Pedigree Complete. I used to have corn flakes then Pedigree Chum.

After breakfast, which takes a maximum of thirty seconds, I am taken outside to the front garden. There I am told to do my business, which I do, but behind the bushes. After that, I am led round to the back garden, in which, during the summer months, I am allowed to roam about, generally doing what I want, when I want. This includes: barking at squirrels, chasing those annoying birds (especially the blue tits from next door - I wonder what they taste like?) and pretty much barking at everything that moves. Oh and then there is Ken, one of my neighbours, to pester. Every time he sees me, I am given two to three biscuits.

However, during winter months I am kept on the chain for a short time on account that I manage to get muddy enough during the summer.

After this, I am taken for a walk and how utterly rude are the people who don't bend down to stroke me? Very!

I don't have lunch, so I drool on my owner's lap, unsuccessfully. I stay inside until Kelsey comes home at half-past three. Until teatime I practise my puppy-dog pout, which is put into action at dinner. I fall asleep at ten-thirty at night.

Kelsey Williams (13)
Birkenhead High School, Wirral

THE SCHOOL BULLY

One day, a young girl called Anna was walking along in the middle of West Kirby woods. Anna was a small girl from South America.

Two minutes after leaving her house, the school bully, Becky, jumped out from behind a bush and yelled, 'Where is Kirsten?'
'I don't know, honestly!' Anna said, trying to protect her best friend.
'I don't believe you!' Becky replied back.
Before Anna knew it, she was surrounded by all of Becky's friends, who were by this time waving their fists at her and telling her to tell them where Kirsten was.
'What do you think you are doing?' Mr Lloyd said in a loud voice.
'We were just messing about Mr Lloyd,' one of the girls said.
There was a long, deafening silence. Suddenly the girls and Becky ran off as they saw Matthew, a short Asian boy with glasses, coming over and they wanted to tease him.

When there was no one around, Mr Lloyd walked over to Anna, picked her up and carried her home. The next day, Becky was kicked out of school for threatening Anna.

Kate Hughes (14))
Birkenhead High School, Wirral

A Diary Of A Cadet

We arrived on the canal bank early on Saturday morning with our life jackets on and wrapped up warm. The water was freezing but the thought of steaming along the canal soon warmed me up. Two boats and six canoes were lined up on the bank ready for us to dive into.

I decided to go pulling as it was a bit chilly for kayaking. I climbed into the boat as it scraped along the bank. We untied it and set off down the calm stretch of water. We passed flocks of swans and baby cygnets. Our oars would often get tangled in the reeds. We passed under many bridges.

On our way back, it started to rain. It bounced off the spare seats in the boats and off the gunwale. As we pulled up along the bank, the waves were splashing against the boat. We tied off the ropes at either end of our boat. I tried to climb out safely, but ended up flat on my face on the bank.

Soaking wet, I jogged over to the shower rooms. I dumped my wet clothes in a bin bag and changed into dry clothes for dinner on the mess deck.

Natalie Hall (14)
Chesterfield High School, Merseyside

A Day In The Life Of Gareth Gates

I would like to step into Gareth Gates' shoes for a day. I know he is a boy and I am a girl, but he has been my inspiration and my idol ever since I read his autobiography. I found out that he got seriously bullied in his secondary school just because of his stammer that he has had from the moment he tried to speak. I can relate to this because I have been bullied in primary school and secondary school just because of the way I look. I feel like me and Gareth have been through a lot of the same emotions because of the bullying.

The first time I saw him was on Pop Idol where it took him twenty seconds to say his name. I didn't think he was going to sing as brilliantly as he did. When the words came out of his mouth, I was so surprised and shocked - this tells me, don't judge people before you meet them!

Another reason for my inspiration in him is that he has got seven A levels. This shows he has worked through thick and thin and still got what he wanted in his life. In one examination for German, he had to sing his answers out.

He is also a role model to many people, and he is only eighteen. He has also achieved all this in a short space of time and he has still got many years to achieve even more.

Amanda Hall (15)
Chesterfield High School, Merseyside

DEAR DIARY

Today was the last day of term. The summer holidays have begun! I can't wait to go to town and hang out with my mates.

We had a disco in school. Everyone from the year went. Charlotte Taylor, Kelly Jones, etc. It was brilliant! I walked through the door and was amazed. The teachers had really splashed out this year! Usually at school discos there would be disgusting food, rubbish music and party games! But this year there was brilliant music, delicious food and *no* party games!

When I arrived at the party, music was booming out of the speakers and the dance floor was packed with people. There were a few people nibbling at the food, but most of my friends were still getting changed out of their dull school uniforms and into their glamorous clothes.

I went over to the food table and started picking at the cocktail sausages when Adam Curtis walked through the door with his big gang of mates all crowded around him. They went and stood in the corner and stared at everyone's dance moves.

Next, my mates came through the door. They all looked so fantastic. I felt like the odd one out. They all went straight to the dance floor and started dancing. I hate dancing, especially at discos. I get so nervous because everyone is looking at you.

Then, Adam Curtis walked towards me with the cutest smile on his face! He asked me to dance! I couldn't believe it! I agreed and it was brilliant!

Helen Gadie (13)
Chesterfield High School, Merseyside

A Day In The Life Of A Car

I was snug, wrapped up in my blanket in the cosy warm garage. Nothing could be heard, just silence. It was so pleasant. Then the normal routine started again. The door was opened, the light was switched on and my blanket was whipped off me. So much for being warm and pleasant. Then it got even colder, my door was opened and a gust of wind came in. I shivered. Then my driver climbed in and switched my engine on. I roared. It hurt because it was early in the morning. 6am for goodness sake. It's not fair, I was enjoying my sleep 10 minutes ago.

So I was on the road. The flashy things were on red. The car next to me looked amazing. It was almost brand new. You could tell it was really well looked after, polished every morning probably. Not like me, all scratched, chipped and dirty. Never mind, I don't care what I look like, I run smoothly and that's all that matters to me and my driver.

Eventually the flashy thing turned green. The car next to me whizzed off at about 80mph. I just chugged along.

We carried on for about another 30 minutes, then we stopped in the usual place. I was surrounded by hundreds of other parked cars. Another gust of wind snuck in as my door was opened again, but it wasn't for long. Then it was shut, my driver walked off and I was left there with all the other cars.

Karen Brimage (12)
Chesterfield High School, Merseyside

Hoofprints In The Snow

The sun was high and the wind was low. A creature rested silent and motionless. The snow was dyed red. Her eyes held no life. The birds sang no song. The leaves were quilted with snow in a calm, mystical atmosphere. The path was invisible.

In the snow, subtle hoofprints rest. The owner is rarely seen. Her mane and tail are pure white and if you catch a quick glimpse, you may only notice her eyes, dark and beautiful as the night, with the stars reflected. Though she was unhappy and lonely, her life seemed blessed. She lived in a faraway land, in which life thrived in an amazing forest, with overlooking mountains that cast immense beauty. Her kindred love is perpetuitive. A rarity so precious that the man who owns her carcass would be extremely wealthy.

Greed dominates our world. Hunters do not care. As they tread on the soft blanket of snow, gunshots fire. Birds flock from the trees in an instant. She never awoke. Silence envelops the land. The hunter took a life; he lived as a millionaire, though he felt no happier. He lived in guilt and greyness.

Alison Dean (15)
Chesterfield High School, Merseyside

THE FAIRY FRIEND

Whisper's fragile, intricate wings fluttered gently through the blue heavens. The world below was just a beautiful green curve. Drawn to it, Whisper dived down.

Under the spreading boughs of a sycamore tree sat a tearful young girl named Daydreamer. Whisper gazed down at her.
'I wish I had a friend,' she mumbled to herself.
Whisper couldn't stop herself. She reached into her tiny pocket for her magic wand and granted Daydreamer's wish. Whisper gazed down and saw that Daydreamer was already giggling with another girl. She looked very cheerful.

Whisper returned to Fairyland feeling pleased with herself, but then however, she began to worry. Fairies weren't actually allowed to grant human's wishes, but surely Sunbeam and Mooncrescent, the fairy king and queen would never find out.

As Whisper reached the Fairyland gates she was stopped.
'Mooncrescent and Sunbeam wish to speak to you!' the guard at the glistening gates screamed at Whisper.
This was not good news. Mooncrescent and Sunbeam only ever wanted to speak to you if you were in serious trouble.

Whisper stepped into the palace and trembled before the king and queen.
'Whisper!' boomed Mooncrescent. 'You have broken two of our very important rules. Firstly, you must never go down to Earth and there is no way that you can . . .'
Whisper interrupted. 'I'm sorry, I can explain, the girl was upset and . . .'
'Enough!' screamed Sunbeam.
'I have no choice but to banish you from Fairyland and that friend you created has been taken away!' roared Mooncrescent.
Whisper fell to the ground, crying. She pleaded, but no good came of it.

Later that day, Whisper sat on the cloud that she had been banished to. She doodled cartoons of Sunbeam and Mooncrescent in her notebook. Whisper decided to fly back down to Earth. Daydreamer was crying

again. Whisper fluttered down through the branches. She began to talk to Daydreamer. Daydreamer looked startled as she gazed at the tiny fairy.
'Do you want me to be your friend?' asked Whisper.
Daydreamer nodded and looked happy, but still shocked.

Daydreamer and Whisper were friends for months. Whisper spread the word to all the fairies and to this day humans and fairies live together in harmony. Sunbeam and Mooncrescent found they could no longer order the fairies around. Eventually Whisper was named the new queen of Fairyland.

Siobhan O'Hagan (12)
Chesterfield High School, Merseyside

DEAR DIARY

Today was my first day at my new school and probably the worst day of my life.

It started okay. I'd got up earlier than usual, actually ironed my uniform, brushed my unruly hair into a loose ponytail and forced a piece of burnt toast down for breakfast.

I left early as well, but to my complete horror, I got lost. After getting directions off an old lady, I arrived at 8.55. Thankfully, I knew where my form room was.

I flew down the corridor, my uncomfortable shoes squeaked on the polished floor and the smell of disinfectant filled my nostrils. I knew my ponytail had come undone and as I burst into the classroom a few girls tittered.
'Hm, Melinda Johnson, isn't it?' the teacher asked gruffly.
I nodded.
'Sit at the back,' she demanded after handing me my timetable. 'You have already wasted enough of my time.'
Oh great. Cruella De Vil is my form tutor, I thought sadly.

The first three lessons before lunch passed in a blur and soon the dinner bell rang. I'd been dreading this bit. Who would I sit and eat with? What if none of the food was vegetarian? Oh no!

I worked myself into such a state that I made a plan to spend lunch in the medical room. Eventually the nurse sent me home. I can't go back tomorrow. I hate it there. I want my old school back. I wonder how I can persuade Mum to move back to Liverpool . . .

Alecia Marshall (12)
Chesterfield High School, Merseyside

A Day In The Life Of Adam
(In the style of James Herbert)

I sat in my garden and watched the world go by. Glorious red clouds merged into pink-grey in the setting sun. The late summer air gliding about me, slapping me around the face and flushing up my nose.

The beauty of the day was apparent to some but not to me. I could tell the flowers were dying in my garden, each petal had a story to tell, some wanted a happy life; others would have been glad to die. I could see the last of the summer birds flying south and hear children saying their farewells as the holidays were over.

I had just finished drinking a glass of wine, the finest, but every good thing must come to an end. I drank bliss.

I was in an unsure state of mind, my leave was over in two days. My wife would be at work tomorrow. I reached into my pocket and pulled a pack of cigarettes out and placed one in my mouth. I looked up at the ever-dying sun; it had almost set and was getting dark. I sat in sorrow thinking of all the things I would have liked to have done; my optimism was over, dying like the echoing rays of light, the rays of my life. I questioned, 'Am I alone?' A tear formed, a tear of corrosive texture, of icy coldness.

My wife Veronica came to sit beside me, holding my hand and I was not alone on this fair night.

Adam Stannard (18)
Cloughside School, Manchester

MELODY'S ACCIDENT

'Here comes Melody!' yelled Amy, running down the stable yard.

The Virginian horse farm was traditional with grain dryers and three big barns, each with six stables in each one.

Amy was fifteen years old with long, thick, dark brown hair and pale pink, freckled skin. Ty and Ben were handsome Irish stable hands, eighteen and nineteen, both with stone-green eyes and pale skin.

An old, green, battered horse lorry had pulled up into the yard and a man in his sixties got out. 'I'm Ray Philips,' he said. 'Thank you for offering to look after Melody.'

The lorry disappeared down the lane. As it rattled, Melody reared up. 'Let her go Amy, she'll go over!' shouted Ty.
She came back down but before Amy could catch her, she took off towards the paddock.
'She's going to try and jump the fence. She won't make it because of her weight - she's pregnant,' yelled Ben.

There was a sudden crack! Amy could see the wood sticking into the mare's side. She shouted to Ben to call the vet. 'Tell him it's an emergency, Ben.'

Five minutes later the vet arrived. He was a young man with bleached hair and sea-blue eyes. 'This is worse than I thought,' he said, taking a closer look. 'Ben get some hot water, some Dettol and lots of cotton wool.'

An hour passed and Scott, the vet, looked up. 'She's going to be fine and so is the foal,' he said.

With relief Melody walked back to the stable. The warmth of the mare reminded Amy how much she loved her.

Tanya Robins (12)
Dulverton Middle & Community School, Somerset

A Day In The Life Of Alice

Monday
Hi, Alice Here. Welcome to my holiday diary! Oh, this is going to be such fun - *not!* I'm here at this horrible holiday camp for kids. I've only been here a day and already I hate it. Also, I'm going to miss my best buddy's three-day birthday sleepover! Oh, *I hate my mum!* I have ended up sharing a grungy cabin with some of the snobbiest girls alive. They took one look at me and stuck their noses so high in the air, they almost got stuck to the ceiling. None of them speak to me and I prefer to keep it that way. Uh-oh, the camp leader is coming round the cabins. Gotta go. Bye!

When I get home I am *so* going to kill my parents! They asked us what activities we wanted to do. I wanted to do footie, but all the other girls voted for sewing. Well, I wasn't having that. I kicked and screamed and kicked some more. I think I went a bit too far but I am doing football this afternoon.

Can't write much. It's too painful. I fell in football and broke two fingers. One of the boys in the other cabins fouled me. Hey, I might get to go home early now. Then I can go to my buddy's birthday party. Gotta go!

Still in pain this evening. The boy who fouled me came over to apologise. I tried to make a rude sign at him but it's very difficult with your fingers strapped together. Oh, hold on, the camp leader's calling me.

I love my mum! She heard that I'd broken my fingers, and being the soppy mum that she is, she's coming to take me home early. Now I can go to my friend's party after all. Mum's here. Must dash. Bye.

This place smells horrible. Disinfectant mixed with hospital food. The doctor's coming. I'm supposed to be resting, not writing in my diary. By the look on my mum's face, it looks as if I'm not going to the party after all. *Ooohh!* I hate my life.

Emma Sorrell (12)
Dulverton Middle & Community School, Somerset

A Day In The Life Of A Soldier In The Second World War

(This is taken from a true story about George D Stickley who was born in Canada and fought during the Second World War. He has since died of bone cancer at the age of eighty-six)
By Emma J Harris, his grandchild

It was a cold, dark, stormy night. The wind felt like knives digging into my heart. The rain felt like bricks and the lightning lit the pathway to death. Being a soldier in the Second World War was hell.

One terrifying day, I was hiding with my best friend. Suddenly a German threw a grenade onto his back. I had to see him get blown up right next to me. But I had to go on. Suddenly a bullet shot the side of my arm. I wrapped a piece of rag from his sleeve around the wound. This was the last thing he could do for me.

After the war I returned to my wife. On that very night I had a dream that I was strangling a wretched old German. But in the real world I was strangling my wife. Fortunately, she managed to wake me up. I will never forgive them for what they did to me and everyone else.

Emma Harris (12)
Dulverton Middle & Community School, Somerset

A Murky Tale

I jumped over the wall, totally ignoring the sign. All I saw was a wood. There were old oak trees, small young beech trees and a small blue stream trickling through the middle. I went up to it and saw a little minnow darting around on the bottom. I looked around. This was such an ordinary wood just like all the others around here.

As I turned around, I felt a strange sensation. I focused on a small, greyish brown patch of mud. There was something strange about it.

I climbed up a tree to get a better view of the place. I stared at the greyish brown patch of mud. I became rigid with fright. The mud began to stir. Something was underneath moving around. I tried screaming but no sound came out.

Something appeared out of the mud. It looked like a finger. Then a whole hand. It was covered in mud. I couldn't move. I couldn't do anything. I tried blinking it away. It crawled out of the mud and started coming towards me. I shut my eyes really tight and screamed.

Next I felt a hand shaking me, I screamed again.
'Are you alright dear?' - it was Mum. 'It's time to get up now,' she said. Then turned and walked out of the door.
All was well. It was only a dream. Well I thought it was - until I noticed the dirty handprint on my pyjamas.

Rosalie Tribe (12)
Dulverton Middle & Community School, Somerset

A Day In The Life Of Michelle Nicholson

6.03am Monday 21st August 2003
This is about me, my mum and now - him.

She has blue eyes and hazelnut hair. She's not really a mumsie type. In my opinion, I'm the parent and she's the child. I have wavy hazelnut hair, emerald-green eyes and I feel as though I look much older than her. Oh - my name is Michelle.

We live in a small flat in the middle of nowhere and there are a few shops, not for teenagers. Our flat is right at the top and down below us, is the freaky Mrs Sunday - she's horrible. She hates children, but near my mum she's as sweet as sugar.

6.05am
The problem is that I think my mum is falling in love . . . I've found out that the man is a computer freak. He has hardly any money, because I checked his wallet, he's not good-looking and he's a loser.

Midday
I pluck up the courage to ask. I say, 'There's this couple going out with each other and someone is jealous. What should that jealous person do?' She replies - after a million years - 'The couple will never forgive that person.'
This strikes me like a bullet in my brain. 'Stop destroying your mum's happiness!'
I obey.

8.00pm, later . . .
She's flirting. I predict that they are going to marry . . . soon. I'll have to put up with him for the rest of my life . . . I think I'm going to cry.

Luchia Pike (12)
Dulverton Middle & Community School, Somerset

How The Unicorn Got Her Horn

In a faraway place there was a little white horse. Her name was Moon. Since she was a little foal she had wished for magical powers. She was never content even though she lived in the most beautiful forest and had everything she wanted.

That night there was a strange light in the sky, but she made her wish as usual and went to bed. However, when she was asleep a magical spark came and spun around her.

In the morning she was devastated to discover that she was no longer the colour of snow, but covered in horrible green slime. She tried to get it off, but it didn't even fade. She was so sad and wished that she was back to normal. She thought how good her life was living in such a beautiful place and how she should have been more grateful.

After a few days something else happened. She was searching for a blue flower when a little fairy appeared out of nowhere.
The fairy said, 'You have learned your lesson, I will now grant you your wish.'

In a flash, the little horse was lovely and white and had a sparkly horn on her head which she found had magical powers. She was now a unicorn. 'Thank you,' she said. 'I will use my new powers well and never be discontented again.'

Paula White (12)
Dulverton Middle & Community School, Somerset

A Day In The Life Of Michael Jackson

It was a beautiful day with the sun shining in my eyes as my chauffeur was driving me to the shopping centre with hoards of fans racing behind. The person sitting next to me was Martin Bashier. He was interviewing me, for my fans to know the way I work and how I act. Today I was going to go shopping for gifts.

I started off in one shop, spending thousands. I could see the place starting to heave with my fans, they were calling my name . . .

Eventually I got out and was being escorted home whilst having questions in one ear and fans screaming in the other. We finally got home and I set off to my hotel.

When I arrived, within minutes, the crowds of people were screaming my name and wanting me to say hello and sign their pieces of paper.

Suddenly after about an hour of saying hello to them, I found myself being overwhelmed by the people who love me so much. They were calling my baby's name and I couldn't resist, so I dangled my baby over the balcony.

They were screaming in fear but I would never do anything to hurt my children. I wished I had never let these TV presenters in as it meant I might be accused of child abuse again. I just wish I had a peaceful life.

Rachael Dale (12)
Dulverton Middle & Community School, Somerset

I Hate My Life - Or Do I?

It was Saturday morning. On the Friday I had been asked to do the annual school cross-country. The problem was I couldn't run! What was wrong with my PE teacher - Oh well.

Let's get on with who I am. I am Hollie Smith, I am 12 years old and I live with my mum and my mum only. I hate my dad. He left my mum just because she was late for dinner one night! First Dad and then the PE teacher - who would be next?

Today was Monday and I had to give in my slip to say that I could do the cross-country. I was amazed that Mum, signed the slip because she knew I couldn't run.

When I got to school, I gave my slip in, with my hands shaking like a mini earthquake on the ground.

In every lesson I was worrying. Finally it was time. I got to the start light.

The man shot the gun . . . I was running . . . but very slowly, it was like running in slow motion, and then nearly at the finish, I realised I was at the front of the crowd . . . had I gone wrong? Then I realised I hadn't gone wrong, I had actually won the race. *Wow!* I was amazed and glad that Mum signed the slip. I can't wait until next year.

Oh I love my life!

Katie Lock (12)
Dulverton Middle & Community School, Somerset

A Day In The Life Of Felix The Cat

I was wiping my whiskers after lapping up my milk, but I was still hungry. Lizzie, my owner, has come to the conclusion that I am too fat, so I am on a diet. Perhaps next door's cat will have some food left over.

I went next door and there it was, staring at me through the cat flap. The golden aim. Mouse heads with tuna chunks in gravy. *Ummm!* It tasted absolutely delicious. I think it was an expensive top quality pouch. I thought, that now with a belly full of grub, I should go and have a lie down. But where? I thought, *at home in the new leather armchair!*

With my belly dragging on the floor, I staggered for the flap. Only realising when I got there, I was stuck!

Frantically pushing against the flap, I heard a big crack. Perhaps if I kept doing this, the whole thing would break. After lots of pushing, I heard another noise. Not a crack this time, but my name. It was Lizzie. She was looking for me. Maybe, If I ran upstairs, and looked out of the window she would see me.

I wriggled up the stairs with a big belly, and while attempting to get to the window, I ripped the net curtain. Stupid thing. Finally, I reached the window, and saw Lizzie. I miaowed at the top of my voice, but it was no use. I would be stuck in here forever!

Joanne Clark (12)
Grittleton House School, Wiltshire

A Day In The Life Of A Baby!

I woke, crying this morning. I don't know why. It annoyed Mum so that was OK and then she had the cheek to moan about getting out of bed. It was 6 o'clock, lazy madam.

She stomped into my bedroom, slung me out of my cot and then gave me a fake smile, pretending she was happy to see me.

I got carried down the stairs in a vigorous way. I thought I was going to be sick. Then, what a change - milk for breakfast! I'm sick of it. I fancied what I could smell my parents eating - a Chinese takeaway, they called it, but I just got milk again last night. They forced it down my neck, so I made sure I was sick all down Mum's back. She wasn't pleased.

I was playing with my toys and then who walked in, Gran - my worst nightmare. She was wearing her floral curtains again.

She came over to me, picked me up, chucked me in the air and pulled my cheeks in different directions. I thought she was going to eat me.

After poking and pulling me, she put me down and my milk reappeared all over the carpet.

Dad is so strange. He just makes funny noises and faces at me and walks off.

After all this excitement I decided it was time for a nap. You'd think that they would have realised that, but I had to scream for about ten minutes.

Bonnie Renicks (14)
Grittleton House School, Wiltshire

A Short Story

Our car pulled up outside the house. My parents had said I'd be surprised. It was more than that; I was astounded! The neighbourhood was silent. Children stopped playing and stared, adults peered out from behind curtains. Our last house didn't really feel special until now. I suddenly found myself feeling shy and out of place, as if I didn't belong.

The house smelt ancient and also had an eerie silence, as if it were dead. There was no light: our windows were boarded up with chipboard and the brown, sixties-style carpets were moth-eaten and worn down.

Mum saw my face, 'Obviously it needs some work doing,' she said.
'It may seem strange at first,' Dad added.
'But you'll get used to it.'
Judging from what I had seen already, that seemed impossible.
'We'll unpack, you go outside and get to know the other children,' my mum suggested.

I walked towards the back door and immediately noticed that the top hinge had come loose. I decided to take the door out to the back garden. That was just as bad; the sky was iron-grey, the pond was murky and the plants drooped so much that the stems were in the shape of an upside-down horseshoe. I remembered my gran telling me a story about upside-down horseshoes. They stood for bad luck. That seemed to be what I was getting most of at that precise moment.

Sarah Halfacree (14)
Grittleton House School, Wiltshire

A Day In The Life Of . . .

I woke to the sickeningly happy banter of the day's shoppers. I was always bemused by the pure ecstasy that the public could achieve from such a monotonous task. This thought barely lingered as I proceeded to prepare myself for the task of the day.

From now until the culmination of the day, I would be attempting to raise any funds possible. I opened my make-do pillow to reveal my pride and joy, my battered guitar. Most individuals would struggle to see past the rustic exterior, but I knew this piece of manufacturing genius could produce my remaining hope of emerging from a dire financial state.

All day I would strum and look, strum and look, with my hopes building with every glance; they would promptly shatter as my head dropped with disappointment. Despite my undying efforts nobody seemed to place more than a penny in my scruffy hat. I had worked all day and for what? Red raw hands and an appetite. My spirits were broken.

I had become accustomed to this feeling by now. Many a day ended in disappointment for me. I was barely sixteen and had lived on this same stretch for what seemed an eternity. Few thoughts passed through my head but I remained a little upbeat as I was not senile just yet! 'Screw 'em!' I said aloud. 'Who needs 'em?'

A glimmer of hope emerged again as I rested down beside my one true friend.

Charles Hamilton (15)
Grittleton House School, Wiltshire

A Day In The Life Of Fred Jones

Fred rolled over to hit his alarm clock into submission and he groaned as he contemplated his day ahead. Several uninteresting pieces of work flashed through his mind as he got dressed and went downstairs. As he went through the ritual of having breakfast, cleaning up and other mundane tasks, he logged onto his school Work From Home initiative from his computer; and seeing the short list of boring assignments waiting for him, he logged off and went out.

As Fred wandered around town, he thought of his absent parents; what they were doing on their business trip, and hoped they would be back soon. He walked around town, seeing none of his friends until lunchtime; then he chatted to them for most of the day.

As soon as he came in, Fred noticed the insistent, high-pitched beep of his computer, calling for him to continue with his studies towards his Solar Education Grade One. Fred reluctantly sat down and began his studies.

As Fred was not particularly intelligent, it took him a while to endure his schoolwork, which included Life Skills. Fred found Life Skills easy, because it had become more and more like simple IT which he liked. Fred mused that with all the recent changes in education, due to space travel, you still could learn French, an archaic language.

It was nearly midnight when Fred finished and he went to bed safe in the knowledge that there was more for him to do tomorrow.

Luke Williams (15)
Grittleton House School, Wiltshire

RHINO RUNS OVER CAR!

Reporter David Watson explains -

One week ago a car was found at the roadside, crumpled and trashed. The police were called in straight away only to find that a rhinoceros had escaped from the local zoo and had run along the countryside, onto the road and hit the car. Two people were killed and three are in hospital, critically ill.

The road on which this ludicrous accident has happened will be shut and many people will be working there through the night.

The rhinoceros was quickly calmed with one shot of a sleeping pallet. Its owner was called in straight away. The manager of the zoo had this to say. 'We are very sorry for the family of the victims. This was a mistake one of our zookeepers made, by not locking the padlock on the door to the rhino's pen, but this mistake has led to terrible deaths and horrible injuries so we are willing to compensate.'

The families of the victims, who do not want to be named, are believed to be taking this case to court. One confident lawyer explained to us that the family has a very strong defence and will probably get a sum of money within the hundred thousand range.

We can only hope that this will not happen again and there will be a close, careful look at many zoos in the country and this zoo will now be closing due to their clumsy and unfortunate mistake.

David Watson (11)
Grittleton House School, Wiltshire

SHORT STORY

It was seven o'clock in the evening and my mum, my dad, my brother and I were driving to Wickfield Park School for an American football match.
'Hurry up Dad,' I said, 'we're going to be late.'
'No we're not,' Mum said, 'kick-off is not until eight.'

We arrived at Wickfield School and I got changed into my kit and went out onto the field. I was playing for Marshfield School.

The ref blew his whistle and the game began. The ball came straight to me. I ran with all my strength up the field until a fat boy tackled me. I threw the ball to one of my opponents.
'That was crap,' someone said.

At the end of the first quarter it was 14-7 to Wickfield.

The second quarter proved more hopeful when we drew level. The third quarter was pants. Wickfield scored two more touchdowns, it was 24-7.

It came to the last quarter and we managed to pull back one touchdown, followed by a conversion which we missed. The ball was passed up field by me and we scored! We were level.
'Who should take the conversion?' somebody said.
'I will,' I called.

I lined out the ball. I stepped back and took the kick. The ball slotted between the posts, the whistle went for full time. We had won!

Samuel Rogers (11)
Grittleton House School, Wiltshire

THE BARN STORMERS

I lined up on the runway with co-pilot Naz Buck in the Winged Wonder or the Wellington Bomber. My base at Boscom Down in Wiltshire was chosen to attack a tank factory at Peenümunde. We were given a green light by the control tower. The engines burst into throaty groans as the power was cranked up to ninety per cent and the parking brake was lifted.

Two-thirds down the tarmac the plane lurched upwards into the setting orange sky.

Forty miles away to port we watched a flock of B17s landing from the daylight raid on Berlin.

By now we were cruising at 20,000 feet going towards the Nazis' homeland.

Suddenly a ME109 shot past the canopy of our aircraft. The gunners in our pack of 10 aircrafts let rip with their special Thompson machine guns. It went down, bursting into flames and falling out of the sky like a ton of bricks.

A voice was heard through the headphones and Pete Knight, our bomb aimer, perked up. The sentence was repeated. 'Open bomb doors. Your bomb marker is red.'

An icy draught tore through the plane. We were shivering in our boots.

By now Pete was looking through the Norton bomb sight in front of me. Strangely there was no flack pounding up at us so we dropped our MK82 load on a path straight into the huge barns containing tanks.

Suddenly the brand new tanks pounded us with armour-piercing ammo' so we limped home on a targeted gunship.

Thomas Crosby (12)
Grittleton House School, Wiltshire

MORE

It was very late at night when I woke up and everything was swallowed in darkness. I jumped violently. A pair of huge purple eyes were staring down at me, deep and mysteriously. I tried to scream, but long fingers closed over my mouth. My eyes were wide with shock and fascination. The fingers released and as the creature stepped back into the half-darkness I saw the figure of what must have been an alien.

Its head was too large compared to its body. It had stick-like limbs, long fingers and knobbly knees. I decided this creature, thin as it was, needed feeding.

Slowly I got out of bed and walked towards it, my heart thumping. I took it by the bony wrist and led it out of the bedroom and along the hall. Nothing like this had ever happened to me before. Where had it come from? A spaceship? No. That was babies stuff.

We reached the kitchen and I opened the fridge, it ate about half the fridge that night. Ham, quiche, anything and after each portion, all it said was, 'More?'

After what seemed like hours, I turned to look at the clock, my feet were getting cold. It was one o'clock.

'I think we should . . .' I started, but when I turned, there was no alien stuffing its face. I searched the dark house but it was gone. Oh well, I wouldn't mind if it were to visit again, even though it ate all the food. All my family had a delicious breakfast at the café down the road that morning.

Lucy Rivers (12)
Grittleton House School, Wiltshire

ALONE

An owl hooted in the darkness and I realised I was alone. Deserted houses stared at me with blank glares and the sky, a black whirlpool, seemed to want to swallow me up.

Moving forward, unsure where my feet would take me, I felt dizzy and my head was throbbing. I looked up and saw a golden, gleaming light. I squinted, only to see the light was moving but no figure was holding it. Curious, I followed. My path was long and winding.

Time passed and I noticed the light descending slowly. In a matter of seconds it was gone. I raced forward and knelt at what looked like a trapdoor. The ground was damp and covered in a sea of gravel. Brushing some away my shivering hand revealed a handle. The handle was metal, rusty and cold to the touch. I tugged at the door, putting all the energy I had into it, slowly but surely the ancient door lifted. I examined the dark passage that appeared before me and lowered myself in.

Reaching the end of the tunnel I heard a smash. The wooden banisters and beams started carrying flames through the passage towards me. I ran. I reached the trapdoor, feeling very triumphant. The door was jammed.

I pulled. The fire was gaining. My hands were swollen. My face was red. It reached me. I tugged frantically and the door jerked open. Seconds later . . . *boom!*

An owl hooted in the darkness and I realised I was alone . . . again.

Roslyn Jackson (12)
Grittleton House School, Wiltshire

THE SEVEN KNIGHTS OF THE GRAIL

Roars echoed around the valley as Ungor, the great Chaos, drew his serrated sword from Ellander, champion of the high elves.

As the evil Chaos roared in triumph, seven remaining knights escaped, planning to retreat to the Ellandrien forest. As they crossed the long-winding river near Nitron they noticed a small village. One of the villagers spotted them and cried out.
'Help us!' he pleaded. 'If the Chaos find us they will destroy us!'
'We shall help,' replied Ellander.
The knights prepared to ambush the Chaos as they crossed the bridge.

Meanwhile the Chaos stormed on, seeking more battles. They crossed the river further upstream and charged into the village . . . only to find that it was empty and had been abandoned.

Enraged, they stormed through the village, searching every building for the helpless villagers. As they stomped around the village, the knights prayed to Elland, destroyer of the greatest evil of all time.

The demon-like Chaos returned to the centre of the apparently deserted village. The nine Chaos turned to leave when suddenly the knights charged, singing Elvin war songs. The Chaos turned too late. Grishna was slain instantly, as was Stormvolt.

The remaining Chaos marched off to a valiant elf. The duels continued, but all were equally matched. Each elf that defeated a Chaos was soon slain himself.

Eventually only Ellander and Ungor were left. 'Back to the shadows, demon,' cried Ellander, dealing the blow to end all evil . . .

After mourning his friends' deaths, Ellander returned to his homeland.

Chris Habgood (13)
Grittleton House School, Wiltshire

A Day In The Life Of The Snowboarding Superhero (Saviour Of The Slopes And Protector Of The Pistes)

After breakfast Zack picked up his drawstring bag and strapped on his snowboard and headed for the slopes.

The mayor was going to open a new run and Zack was going to try it out.

Zack had started snowboarding when he saw someone in the trees. A man was tying the mayor to a snowmobile. Without hesitation, Zack undid his drawstring bag which opened up into a large piece of material. He put the bandanna inside on to cover his hair and sunglasses on so no one would recognise him. He put the drawstring bag material around his neck (as a cloak).

That's why I haven't told you what he looks like, it would give away his secret identity. Zack is a superhero!

Zack saw the snowmobile being driven down the mountain. He started following it, dodging skiers and snowboarders. Suddenly it disappeared into the trees. Zack was gaining on it while dodging trees, so the snowmobile went back on the piste.

By now Zack had caught up. He grabbed a nearby skier's pole and cut the mayor's ropes with it. The mayor fell off the snowmobile before it went over the cliff. Zack followed. The kidnapper grabbed hold of Zack who then pulled a drawstring in his cloak which made it act like a parachute. When they landed the police took the kidnapper away and before the mayor could thank Zack, he disappeared.

Drew Richardson (12)
Grittleton House School, Wiltshire

THE SIREN (CHAPTER 5)

'James, you've forgotten your books,' shouted Mr Thornton.
James ran back to the cottage to collect his books.
'Have a good first day at school,' called Mr Thornton.

James arrived at school. He didn't have many friends because other evacuees had gone to different schools in the area.

Soon it was lunchtime and the bell was just about to go for the children to eat their sandwiches, but instead of a bell, an air raid siren was sounding from the station in the village.

James and his classmates were screaming and running around. It was mayhem, they knew what was coming.
'Calm down everyone, climb under your tables and stay calm,' said the teacher.

All around people were rushing about, James could hear screams coming from all over the place. His new friend, who was also an evacuee from Newcastle, was crying in the corner. He tried comforting her but it was no use.
'Am I going to die?' wailed Susan.

James knew a bomb was going to hit any second. He could hear some children crying, shouting, praying and some were just hunched up on the floor waiting for the bomb to hit.

Suddenly the siren stopped and Mrs Pike asked everyone to put on their jumpers and walk outside. James could hear teachers still shouting, 'Evacuate!'

Immediately after going outside James heard a deafening noise, a tremendous bang and felt an earth-moving tremor. Everyone wailed with fear.
'It's the bomb, it's hit the school.'

Jessica Carwardine (13)
Grittleton House School, Wiltshire

THE UNICORNS

'Grandpa, please will you tell me about the unicorns before I go to bed?'
'Very well, but then you must go to bed.

The legend says that the unicorns used to run wild and free in their forest, not caring about the outside world and just taking care of the animals, until one day a great horn sounded. It was the hunters, but this time they didn't want the foxes or rabbits, they wanted the unicorns.

They were forced out of their forest, over deserts and seas until they came to a place they had never ever imagined - Antarctica.

Everywhere around them was snow and they realised that there was no other life on the island, so by the magic in the unicorns' horns they created life on Antarctica.

From the snow all around came penguins and polar bears and from the sea, whales spouted high into the sky.

They made an oath to look after Antarctica and its creatures and stop man from destroying it as he had done to their forest. But you cannot see them because their coats are as white as snow, but if you look at the highest mountains in Antarctica at night you will see them watching over their precious land.'

Jodie Cleeves (13)
Grittleton House School, Wiltshire

A Day In The Life Of Marvellous Monte

Hamster clippings! I wish that I never had whiskers. They get drenched in water when I go for a drink, they itch my soft ginger fur when I clean myself and they always block my view. They call me Marvellous Monte, the great escaping hamster. I live in a pet shop with other pets like myself and I'm waiting for the day when a human comes along to buy me.

I'm not called Marvellous Monte, the great escaping hamster, for nothing though. I always escape from my cage.

Last week when the shopkeeper was cleaning my cage, I leapt out the second he opened the door. I fell onto the floor with an enormous *bang*, climbed to my feet, galloped to the door and, gasping for breath, I attempted to go under, but I didn't fit. I was too fat!

The ground then began to shake. I turned around just in time to see a pair of cupped hands charging towards me. My feet suddenly had a mind of their own, they lifted off the ground, began to speed under the man's hands, past his feet and *whack!* a gigantic red thing towered over me, killed the light and trapped me in complete darkness. Soon after, the red thing raised and I was welcomed to familiar surroundings, my cage. Mission failed. Diet starts tomorrow.

Laura Bailey (13)
Grittleton House School, Wiltshire

A Day In The Life Of A Child Miner

Gran told me a story about a monster in the mines, who eats or kills little girls. 'He's also completely transparent!' warned Gran.
Apparently, I once had a sister called Emily who was eaten in the mines.

I was scared, but I had to go because Father had coal dust in the chest. Mother gave me a candle, wished me luck and I went.

At the mine Mister Thomas gave me instructions. He said, 'You'll be a trapper, keeping air out of the barrow-way and opening these doors for coal carts with this string.'

He then left me in the dark. I had a candle, but no matches. I strained my eyes by peering into the darkness, hoping there was someone there, but it availed me not.

I suddenly began to feel sleepy and toppled over onto the track, fast asleep.

Later, I forced my eyes open, as I could feel the track trembling. There was a cart coming! I quickly wrenched my body off the track and opened the doors. Now I knew how the monster killed little girls, but not how he ate them . . .

After a few more hours, I saw a thick yellow cloud of smoke. I thought I could even see teeth! That meant it was . . . 'Gas!' I screamed and made a bolt for the exit. As I got to the exit I heard a muffled explosion, an ear-piercing scream, then nothing but total silence.

Georgina Clark (12)
Grittleton House School, Wiltshire

CHOCOLATE BANNED

Head of the Health Society, Mr Bank and the Prime Minister of the UK have introduced a ban on chocolate, sweets, biscuits and crisps, according to health risks.

Tony Blair, the Queen and the Health Society have outlawed the production and consumption of the foods above. Obesity and rapidly declining health are just a couple of the reasons why.

We have interviewed some of the public in Swindon and London to hear their views.

'Fatty foods are disgraceful, it serves you all right,' Mary Summers, child in London.

'I hate the way children think it's right to eat these foul foods,' Mr Sackton, Swindon.

Others do not agree: 'Just a little of what you like, once in a while, surely can't be bad,' Joseph Stone, child in Swindon.

'First our food, then our freedom! They just want control over us,' Mrs Jacqueline, London.

Mr Banks believes:

'This will introduce a new way of eating and living. Of course there will be plenty of money saved also, which will go towards schools and hospitals.'

After a large poll in London, votes are clearly against the ban, but the powers-that-be are decided.

Whether the people will rise up against them or not is unclear but whether we will all go without chocolate is certain.

So, quickly devour your last morsel of sweetness and hope this ban will not last.

Eve Lewis (13)
Grittleton House School, Wiltshire

THE MAGICAL MEDICINE OF TIME
(Based on the Harry Potter books)

'Come on you four,' shouted Mrs Plum, 'you'll be late.'
Paul, Chris, Amy and Tina got up and started packing to go to school.
'Come on, come on, you'll be late,' shouted Mrs Plum again.

Once they had finished eating breakfast Mrs Plum had organised some taxis for them to travel into the station. Once they arrived they asked the way.
'Right then, you get on the train at Platform Ten which is heading right past the canteen, okay?' Mrs Plum explained.

They got on to the train and it pulled out of the station. When they arrived at school they were sent to their dormitories.

The first day at school started smoothly. They had double potions, then herbology and transfiguration. In potions all the children were really bored. Their teacher was Mr Slugwart.

After potion classes, Paul showed them something which he found on the floor. 'Let's travel to Mars,' Paul said.
'Mars!' Amy said.
'Yeah, let's travel to Mars, back in time,' Paul said.
'We need the ingredients,' said Chris.
'I know just where to go,' said Paul, 'Slugwart's office.'
'Let's do it tonight,' replied Amy.

They crept along to Slugwart's office and fetched the ingredients. They used the invisibility coat to get there.
'We've got them, let's get back,' said Tina.

They got back and started making the potion to drink which would make them go back in time to Mars.

Then Mr Slugwart entered . . . 'What are you doing with these ingredients of mine, hey . . .'

Adam Longhurst (13)
Grittleton House School, Wiltshire

ANGOLIA'S QUEST

'Salugar the great demon is known to live in the Emblius Forest. He lives by burning travellers and consuming their ash. He is known to be a great horned, dragon-like creature, but with a bear-like body,' said Master Giyuka.
Angolia screamed, 'When I'm older I'm going to banish Salugar to Hell, like my father tried five years ago.'
'Brave words Angolia, I hope you do.'

Fifteen years later Angolia decided to fulfil the words that he had spoken when he was five.

Later, in his hut, he was sharpening his sword and thinking about his father. Then he picked up his father's tarnished armour and put it on. A perfect fit!

He set out. It was dark and dingy, suddenly he saw a flash of light and heard a great roar. He ran towards the light. It must be Salugar, he thought. Then he saw Salugar, feeding on some smoking ash.

Then, as quick as a flash, Angolia rushed into the clearing and jumped up in the air, ready to strike. Salugar flew up and went into a frenzy of fire. Angolia ran behind a rock, checking for weak spots he could pierce with arrows. The only ones were the wings. Then he loaded his bow with several arrows and fired them into Salugar's right wing. As fast as a blink he fell to the floor in pain.

Angolia took his chance and sliced off his head.

Jonathon Shergold (12)
Grittleton House School, Wiltshire

A Day In The Life Of Amy Greenaway

Amy Greenaway was a girl who lived with her wealthy family about two hundred years ago.

On sunny day she went for a walk, further than usual, to the other side of the park and out of the gates. In front of her she saw a tall, black factory. Through the window and in the yard she saw lots of children. She remembered that her father owned this factory.

As she went closer to the building, she saw a girl coughing and sneezing wearing old rags. Amy thought to herself that this was terrible. There was lots of smoke everywhere.

She could hear shouting and slashing of a whip on the children who were screaming. Amy walked over to the man with the whip, snatched the whip off him and shouted to him that he must never treat these poor children like that again.

Amy felt so sorry for the poor girl, who was ill, that she took her home with her when Amy's mother saw them she gave the girl some hot soup, a bath and clean clothes.

Amy spoke to her father as soon as he came home. She told him what she had seen that day, and how upset she was at the way the children were treated. Amy's father truly didn't realise what was happening and quickly put things right.

Amy had had an extremely eventful day. She had made a new friend and helped many children have a better life. She went to bed very happy.

Katherine Trim (13)
Grittleton House School, Wiltshire

GAINS AND LOSSES

He picked up the official-looking letter from the War Office and his heart thumped. His mind raced as he thought about what had happened in the last twenty-four hours.

James Scolfield had been sitting on a plush chair inside his favourite restaurant, excited but incredibly nervous about what he was going to do. Dan, his younger brother, had a way of calming nerves but he was away fighting a war, somebody else's war.
He looked at Julie who was looking back at him quizzically. She blinked and said, 'A penny for your thoughts?'

Without thinking twice he started his proposal to her.
She smiled back at him lovingly and said, 'Yes.'

James had fallen asleep that night a very happy man. The next morning he lay thinking for a whole hour, which was unusual for him, as he was a very active person. Firstly he thought of his future with Julie. Then he thought about the delight on his brother's face when he would hear that there was going to be a wedding. Dan always enjoyed celebrations.

The thought of his parents though, saddened him; they would have got on so well with Julie.

His mind suddenly came back to the present, the letter, heavy in his hands, had to be opened. Slowly he slit the envelope and unfolded the sheet, it read:-

'We regret to inform you that your brother, Dan Scolfield, has been killed in action. He died serving his country.'

Guy Pilbeam (14)
Grittleton House School, Wiltshire

SEEING IS BELIEVING

The full moon rose and its rays pierced through the misty clouds, over the dark tower block which glowed like forgotten Christmas tree lights. Flashes of colour glared on the streets below, and umbrellas protected the fleshy shells underneath them, from snow falling from the bloated sky . . .

A man lies in his bed dreaming of things to come; nightmares of murder and suffering, and dreams of love and lust plague him through the restless hours of his sleep. But this time it's different.

Al lay there in an unconscious slumber between this world and the next, and out of the darkness of these dreams he sees, he sees, Wanda his wife lying there dead, next to a car shattered against the wall, on the frozen snow, with her blood tainting the snow red. A man runs to her and picks her bloody, broken head up, then in her bosom, cries an endless cry.

Al woke up with a cold shudder and drips of frozen sweat on his face. He lay there for hours staring at the same space of wall and wondering if what he saw was just his mind playing tricks on him again. He staggered down the gloomy hallway thinking of what he had just seen and weeping under his breath. He looked to the right and saw his small metallic kitchen and then it blurred and he could see an operating theatre, with his wife on the table, and a small beep, another one, another one and then silence.

Alexander Bailey (14)
Grittleton House School, Wiltshire

THE FINAL DESCENT

A car sped into the airport car park. Eric stepped out into the frozen night's air, his warm breath clouded around, Jimmy his son, was four, they were going on holiday for the first time.

Eric lifted the suitcase from the boot and with Jimmy's hand he walked across the car park, their feet crunching in the frosty silence. Jimmy's excitement was infectious and Eric found himself looking forward to their trip too.

They took their seats just before the huge wheels started rolling down the runway. It was like a washing machine whirling faster and faster, until they left the runway and the chattering started again.

They had just finished eating when the reek of acrid smoke crept into the cabins. Soon a grey haze hung over them.
'An error has occurred, everything will resume as usual soon.'

Two minutes later:
'Could everyone put their life jackets on and take the brace position for an emergency landing.'

By now everyone could see smoke hanging in the sky from the direction of the engine. The engine started to choke. There was a jolt, the plane started to dip. Fear swept through the plane like a bad smell, as everyone's stomachs were turned upside down by the speed and force as the plane dived. Down and down it went. The sea almost opened up ready for it. Then the waves crashed over, covering all traces.

Alexandra Black (14)
Grittleton House School, Wiltshire

EMBERS

Sunday 4.30am, market day. Bridge Street was full of hasty stallholders eager to trade. The street also housed a small orphanage. Inside all was quiet.
'Get up you lazy tykes!' howled Miss Thorn. She was a spinster at 59. Her face was a story in itself, her hair was like withered string. Worn, ill-fitting clothes draped over her scrawny frame.

The orphanage wasn't much better. The rugged floorboards, peeling paint and the vile smell were among the makings of the hell hole.

The cane was thrashed across the floor. 'Get up!'

The whole house reeked of stale smoke from Miss Thorn's cheap cigarettes. She had ignored the fact that smoking would kill her one way or another. She had left a cigarette smoking downstairs as usual while she made the orphans' lives hell for the next few minutes. What she didn't know was that her dog Tyson had knocked it out of its ashtray, leaving it on the floor to burn. Of course it wasn't noticed. It was a familiar smell. Miss Thorn, as usual, directed the children to do their chores (scrub every inch of the house).

It wasn't until Tyson ran up the stairs followed by fire that anyone knew there was something undoubtedly wrong.

Panic arose, everyone knew that the old place would go up like a tinderbox. Stallholders below watched flames rip through the house. Screams from terrified orphans rang in their ears, but nothing could be done.

Jasmine Lewis (13)
Grittleton House School, Wiltshire

Gold

'Land ahoy!' shouted the captain. Weeks of constant struggle had finally paid off. They had found the lost island of Gold.

Suddenly the magnificent ship hit the sharp cliff of the last Skull. 'Abandon ship!' screamed the captain.

Water was gushing into the gaping hole in the side of the boat. The cliff ate away at its prey. The sharp teeth dug into the wooden flesh. Its assistants gutted the inside. The crew fled their pride and joy. The boat sank gallantly into the pearled sea. Soon the ship was lying on the seabed.

The crew members slowly ascended the beach, scarred and battered, baking in the heat. The men began to search the emerald island for their long-awaited treasure, when they stumbled across more than they had bargained for. They had found a lost tribal settlement.

At first the tribesmen were cautious of them. They jutted their spears towards the crew members' necks and circled around them like vultures. After a lot of begging and persuasion the pigmies finally removed their spears from the crew members' throats. They then led them to their village.

There they stayed for four weeks searching for their beloved treasure. The crew members became friendly with the little black men. They built up trust and a strong bond of friendship.

One misty morning when the grass was jewelled and the fire was dead, they set off on their treacherous journey. After days of searching, the moment had finally come, they were overjoyed! They had found the gold!

Matthew Mumford (13)
Grittleton House School, Wiltshire

THE TRAGEDY

We had been looking forward to the school skiing trip for months. All of us had been saving hard and been shopping to get all of the clothing we needed. As it was our last year this would be our last school trip and we hoped it was to be the best ever. That night as the bright sun went down behind the glittering snow-covered mountains we felt very excited.

On the first morning we ran down for breakfast and when we had finished we got put into our groups. We collected our skis, as we were very close to the slopes so we walked. We were bursting with excitement and for many of us it was our first time skiing.

The following day we progressed up the mountain. To get there we took a 'bubble' that could hold four people. We were all having an amazing time and our skiing was improving all the time.

On the third morning we set off up the slopes and I felt a bit uneasy as I looked up the mountains.

Suddenly there was an immeasurable explosion. The top of one of the mountains had broken off and a sea of snow came hurtling down the piste. The better skiers were swallowed up in the snow as they had been higher up. As we were in the bubble all we could do was look down on the tragedy.

Victoria Rich (14)
Grittleton House School, Wiltshire

The Voice That Made A Difference

The room is a warm, safe haven. The ancient stone fireplace is stacked with coal and is emitting a tremendous heat. It hisses gently like a snake and crackles like a spark of lightning in a storm. The warm atmosphere envelopes me as I sink lower in my grandma's old, comfy armchair. I start to feel drowsy and the sounds of the television begin to fade.

I gaze out of the window. The moon in the star-filled sky is shrouded in an eerie mist. Everything is still. A sweet aroma overwhelms my senses and an owl is hooting in the distance.

I look out across the lake. The surface is a mirror reflecting the sky, I feel relaxed. I notice a silhouetted figure moving; it is darting between the trees. It seems to be getting closer. Then I hear it . . . a friendly, familiar voice. I know it from the past but can't put a face to it. A nervous feeling creeps up my spine.
The voice says, 'Don't be afraid Layla, I'm here to help you. I know you are being bullied at school,'
'How do you know I'm being bullied?' I interrupt, cautiously.
'I am your guardian angel. You must tell a teacher Layla, don't let the bullies get to you.'

As I start to respond another voice is calling me;
'Layla, Layla, wake up!' I open my eyes and my grandma is standing in front of me looking anxious.
'Your teacher is here to see you!' she says . . .

Rebecca Crisp (13)
Hardenhuish School, Wiltshire

BIN LADEN FOUND DEAD IN FLAT

Reported by Max Clilverd.

Yesterday, the 18th of March at three o'clock local time, the world's most wanted terrorist - Osama bin Laden, at forty-six years of age, was found dead in a flat in Lahore, Pakistan. The body had a gunshot wound in the temple. The death was thought to have been suicide.

Bin Laden's flat was raided after a policeman on duty heard a gunshot from the street outside.

'I heard a gun so I went to check it out with three other officers, and there we found him,' the policeman stated. 'His flat was laced with guns and explosives, mostly illegal. He also had almost three hundred grams of ecstasy, they are now with the FBI.'

This will be a very big burden lifted off George Bush and the American authorities' shoulders.

'The world is a safer and not as threatening place with this man dead.' A cold but true statement from George Bush, the American president.

Tony Blair will also be relieved that Osama bin Laden is now dead. At a press conference yesterday he stated, 'I am now finding it easier to handle world events with him off mine and many other's backs.'

Bin Laden, the co-ordinator of the September the Eleventh attacks. Also leader of terrorist group Al Qaeda, will be highly missed by them.

But is this the end of Al-Qaeda? 'No probably not. This group of terrorists is at such a great number, it is hard to stop them,' said the Home Secretary, David Blunkett.

With these events, it is always hard to beg the question, what is the next step? Colin Powell, the American Home Secretary stated, 'This is a very good day for the war on terrorism. This is a big leap closer to peace in the Middle East and also in the United States of America. But it is not over and if we keep on fighting the way we are now, this war on terrorism will soon be gone.'

Max Clilverd (13)
Hardenhuish School, Wiltshire

SPACECRAFT SEEN IN PARK?

Reported by Emily Tudgay

On the 23rd March a UFO was said to have been seen by Sarah Jones.

The 23-year-old was walking home from the bus stop after work and saw a light in the sky, she carried on walking but the light got brighter and seemed to be following her.

She waved down a passing car and spoke to the driver Mr Blane, who said, 'A spacecraft landed in the park. It was big with windows around the edge, it was very bright and had a metal door.'

Sarah Jones continued, 'A figure came out, it was a tall creature and had a green body. His arms were long and he had yellow bulging eyes.'

When Sarah Jones got home after this incident she rang up the police and reported it. The police then got in touch with a group of investigators and took them to the scene where the UFO was said to have landed. They were looking for any evidence that could have been left behind from the spacecraft.

The investigation team said that there were some marks on the ground that could have been made by the spacecraft. The police had found some unexplained objects in the bins that were glowing. They took them away to be analysed.

Mr Hains, in charge of the investigation, says, 'This is the most uncommon thing that has happened through my years of working with this team. We have never had a situation as serious as this. We have looked at the items found and can tell you that they were left from the spacecraft.'

We are appealing to the general public to come forward with any more evidence or details about this amazing discovery.

Emily Tudgay (12)
Hardenhuish School, Wiltshire

ROT IN PEACE

Jon Day reports from Manchester

Murderer dead in a canal

Richard Hillman, the Manchester murderer, committed suicide last night by driving his family car into a canal.

Hillman, 55, drove the car at about 80mph into the canal whilst his wife and her children were tied up in the back seats.

Early reports suggest that Hillman took the family from their North-East Manchester home, tied them up and then drove away from their home, shocking local people. A brief streetcar race took place as three locals saw Hillman drive away from their house garage.

Hillman's wife Gail said he came back, not for revenge, because he wanted the family to die together with him.

In a press conference, she also told of her frightening experience underwater. 'I managed to free myself from the car before I was rescued.'

The rescuer was Hillman's neighbour who didn't want to give his name. He said, 'I didn't know Richard that well to know what he did. I tried to rescue him but I couldn't find him.'

Hillman was a very popular . . .

Turn to pages 3 & 4

Jon Day (13)
Hardenhuish School, Wiltshire

CAVE OF DARKNESS (CHAPTER ONE)

Issac ventured on as little Imp tagged along on a collar and lead. Imp was three foot high, with grey skin, a long nose, black beady eyes and upon his back lay two black wings. Imp had been captured many years ago and was now the property of Isaac. The teenager had long dark brown hair covering his red, devilish eyes and his mouth was almost a scar. Isaac was an adventurous boy and a loner. Imp hated Isaac and just wanted to be with his own kind.

A smile crossed Isaac's face. He stood in amazement peering at the majestic sight. Cobwebs hung from each corner of the cave. Darkness was all to be seen past the jagged rocks at the cave entrance.

Once Isaac had gotten over his state of excitement, he searched in his pocket until he found his light stone. Switching it on, Isaac was content. Entering the cave, Isaac wasn't sure what to feel, fear or joy?

Isaac and Imp went far into the dark where the air was hot and stuffy, oxygen low, all of the entrance had disappeared now, but Isaac hadn't noticed and didn't care.

Imp wasn't at ease being dragged along; shapes seemed to be watching everywhere. He squealed, started hopping from one foot to the other, flapping his wings in an agitated way. Isaac stopped; Imp's actions worried him, now panic-struck, as he could see no way out. Suddenly Isaac felt cold steel enter his skin, his face pale as death . . .

Joseph Doliczny (12)
Hardenhuish School, Wiltshire

ALIENS LAND ON EARTH

On Friday 21st March 'aliens' landed on Earth at Lacock Abbey. The leader of the aliens, Minfee has told us, 'We mean no harm, do not be alarmed.'

It is hard not to be alarmed as these seven aliens have three shocking blue eyes, purple lips and spit, vibrant green and orange hair and long, thin necks.

The aliens arrived in the early hours of the morning in a oval-shaped spaceship.

Lisa Bush was there when the aliens made their first appearance.

and she quoted, 'I was truly amazed when I saw their spaceship land. Shortly after the aliens held up one of their four legs and appeared to wave.'

All of the aliens are almost identical apart from Minfee who has a longer neck.

Reporter Kate Ellis interviewed Minfee and Peefee, the youngest.

'Question one, why did you come to Earth?'

Minfee replied, 'We have a song that might answer your question. The song is: A spaceman came travelling on a ship from afar, 'twas light years from time since their mission did start, and over a town he halted his craft, and it hung in the sky like a star . . .'

'Question two, what is your mission?'

'To collect five clouds,' Peefee said.

'Question three, why do you need five clouds?'

'Because we have no water on our planet Zog. Five clouds will last at least ten years. We will leave tomorrow at midnight and will collect 100 stars. Thank you ever so.'

Kate Ellis (12)
Hardenhuish School, Wiltshire

SCIENTISTS DEVELOP BLUE SKINNED PEOPLE

With years of planning and researching, scientists have finally reached their goal of creating blue-skinned people.

They have larger quantities of water in their bodies and therefore they weigh 3 stone more than average people.

These strange creatures are not really human but are related more to Martians on the planet of Mars. This was proved when a 26-year-old man was almost identical to a Martian found on Mars 3 days ago

A scientist says, 'We were so astonished we could hardly breathe.'

Mrs Jones from Liverpool says, 'It's changed my life, I don't feel nearly as blue.'

Mrs Green from Sheffield replied with a more negative comment, 'It's preposterous, you should be inventing teleporters.'

Scientists predict in thirty years, all the world's people will be blue-skinned and look similar. This is good because there will be no more racist comments about black and white people.

Blue-skinned people also have a special digestive system which dissolves food, so there will be no more toilet!

Chris Munden (12)
Hardenhuish School, Wiltshire

THE MYTH OF THE ZIZZER

The zizzer flies, the zizzer walks. The zizzer runs, she'll kill her victims in seven different ways. Furiously slices your head off with her mantis arms. Impaled on her killer spikes. Claw through the head from her eagle claws. Weirdly hypnotised by the bloodshot eyes, and a poisonous blow from the scorpion tail. Sliced and diced by the diamond-edged, sabre tooth, scissor teeth. Brutally bludgeoned by the bull-like horns. Or dropped to death into a canyon, screaming as you go.

Beware the zizzer with the jaws that bite and swipe. Travel through the huge forest of spines and never come out the other side.

Never get stood on by a talon. Watch out for the bat wings that sing your death song. Avoid the arms that harm and charm. Beware of the horrible horns that push and pull.

The zizzer rises for 20 moons. Then goes back to the depths of where it came, nonetheless she rises again in three hundred years time. She will kill one hundred victims before she rests. Only one thing can kill the mighty zizzer and that's the great grandson of Zeus. Beware the zizzer flies, the zizzer walks and the zizzer runs. Fear the zizzer!

Chris Lewis (12)
Hardenhuish School, Wiltshire

HE CAVES IN, IN THE END

The world's most wanted man, Osama bin Laden, was arrested yesterday evening by British troops in Afghanistan. The troops were on a training mission in preparation for a possible war on Iraq.

The lieutenant of 43 Para was parachuting out of the helicopter when he spotted some movement in one of the higher caves. When he landed he told the commander and he sent troops in. This is what the commander said. 'We certainly surprised him as he thought he was safe from us finding him as his cave was high and dark. When we arrested him we noticed there was a blue kit bag with objects stored inside.'

The troops searched the bag and found several links to Al Qaida bases and leaders. They also found, what looked to be a bag of anthrax, but that has been sent to a science lab to be examined.

Bin Laden is currently being questioned by US and British forces.

President Bush made a speech yesterday after he was told the news, these are some of the contents of the speech.

'It has been a hard and long search but we have eventually found this evil terrorist who will never see another street, town or city.' Bush continued, 'It is more than likely that he will be executed by the electric chair with many happy and eager viewers. With a possible war with Iraq we cannot get too over confident at this moment in time.'

David Brown (12)
Hardenhuish School, Wiltshire

A Day In The Life Of... My Cat

Greetings fellow feline friends! Haribold here, or as my owners miaow: Sidney... call me Sidney (Sid for short).

10.45pm: The day's begun! My brother Marlin (owners miaow 'Max' Max. Interesting name...) is searching for delicious mice. Never catches any. Put downstairs I will rest... peaceful rest...

2am: I fancy searching - not for mice, since I gave up mice for Litren. (Owners miaow 'Lent')... farewell...

5am: I thought I would miaow about seeing my tabby lady cat friend Nancy. *Purrr*... Nancy makes me purr. She was searching as well - and had caught one mouse! Congratulations Nancy! *Purrr.* (I come back just to miaow about seeing Nancy! Love-struck.

6.30am: Stopped searching now. Realised I went searching too late! The rotten mouse I ate before Litren has affected my brain. (Not the reason I gave up mice for Litren... well... maybe it is...) perhaps I should rest...

8am: Mouses of Milton! I have just been disrupted by humans taking me upstairs! Trying to rest again now, after that rude disturbance!

12pm: Need to sleep now, proper sleep. Goodnight! Don't let the little mice bite!

4pm: Woken again! Scary ring and big vibrations from the human flap! Human kitten came into our house. I miaowed and came to investigate! Sniff... definitely one of ours! Back to sleep again...

9pm: Miaow! I'm feeling wild! I play with my swaying tail! Now I'm dizzy...

I will invite my lovely, smelly material to play with me. I see mice. Where are they now? Too dizzy...

10.45pm: Recovered from evils material's affect. Sleep time...

Jessica Davies (12)
Hardenhuish School, Wiltshire

DAY IN THE LIFE OF ANNE FRANK

Tuesday 18th August 1944

Last night was horrifying, it was like a nightmare even though I was fully awake. All I could hear was gunfire from planes and guns. Then the footsteps, which, every time I heard them, were like thunder that will one day kill me, like it has done so many others right in front of my eyes. Although so many surround me I am so alone, so cold, not to mention so hungry. Yet I still have hope in my heart that some day I will be rescued and this cruelty will be ended, and I can be with my family once again.

Tuesday evening 18th August 1944

During today I ripped my dress, the navy blue one with white and purple flowers, which Mother bought for my birthday party last summer. I got it caught on some barbed wire.

I had the most happy daydream today, it was Father, Mother, me and the rest of the family all on a summer picnic laughing, singing all having fun, in a beautiful green field out in the meadow! Now having images like this one is the only thing keeping me alive and hopeful at this time in life. Perhaps Hitler will have a change of heart and bring this time of suffering, death and his dictatorship to an end.

Dayna James (13)
Hardenhuish School, Wiltshire

A Day In The Life Of A Robin

I woke up on a joyous spring morning. The grass was waving in the wind and a radiant sun was rising on the horizon. I dived out of my nest, which was high up in a sycamore tree on a pleasant old farmer's field, spread my wings and soared over the land. I visited the farmhouse where a little old lady lays bread out on the bird table and hangs feeders from the old cherry tree at the end of the garden. Today there were hazelnuts, all golden brown, my favourite.

I was happily tucking into a stale piece of seasoned bread when I heard a loud caw from behind. I turned to see a large, jet-black rook hurtling towards me, talons pointed. I fell out of the tree in fright, but managed to pull up before colliding with the ground. I raced away as fast as I could with the rook on my tail feathers. Him being more cumbersome than me, I darted off into a twisted oak tree, turning this way and that, trying to lose him, but he carried on chasing.

Then I saw a small hole amongst the dense branches. I just managed to squeeze through. The rook tried to follow me, but knocked himself senseless on the branch. He spiralled to the floor in a heap of feathers. I flew back to my nest, exhausted, picking off the odd worm on the way.

Chris Young (13)
Hardenhuish School, Wiltshire

A Day In The Life Of An Evacuee

I woke up to a dark and rainy day. It looked almost as dismal as me. I wished this day had never come. I felt terrible. Slowly, I climbed out of my bed and crossed the unadorned wooden floor, to my chest. As I searched clumsily through, looking for my 'Sunday best' dress, I heard Mama calling me,
'Come on Harriet, the train will have gone without you if you're not quick!' I was going to point out that I wanted it to go without me, but I decided not to.

I pulled on my clothes and went to say goodbye to our cat, Ginger. As I stroked her velvety coat I felt a large tear roll down my face, I covered my eyes in an attempt to stop the next one from coming, but it still came and another after it and another, until my face was like salty waterfalls. I left Ginger playing with her toy mouse.

I walked down the stairs, dragging my feet as I went.
'Come on Harriet, you'll wreck your new shoes if you keep on doing that,' nagged Mama.
'I know, I just don't want to go,' I replied.
'It will be OK, you'll see,' Mama said comfortingly. 'It's time to go now.'

I picked up my bag, walked out of the house and along the road to the station. The train was waiting for me. I climbed on and said goodbye to the things I knew.

Hannah Jones (12)
Hardenhuish School, Wiltshire

WHEN PIGS FLY

How many times have you ever said, 'When pigs fly'? Well now if you say that you mean yes, because last month Professor Edward Smith discovered an extraordinary pig who can fly!

An eye witness, Terrance Williams, 62, from Wiltshire, Had this to say, 'I was just picking my beans in my back garden, when I heard a noise, so I looked upwards and there was this big fat pink thing flying overhead, I was terrified.'

Another eye witness, Geraldine French, 79, told us this, 'At first I thought it was just a child's balloon, but when I was putting my washing out I heard a really loud snort, I was horrified to learn it was the 'balloon'. I reported my sighting to the police.'

Seventeen other sightings of the pig were reported to the police.

Eugene Harris, a fisherman from North Wiltshire, caught the flying pig in his fish net, on instructions from his friend, James Phillips, a detective in the North Wiltshire police force, who was fishing with him and heard the situation on his radio.

When they dissected the pig it was hollow, other than a bird's dead body.

Scientist Andrew McGregor told us earlier that this was believed to be a *scam* from one of the local butchers, Fred and Elliott's to sell more of their famous bacon.

The manager was sentenced to a year's imprisonment and three months of Community Service because we all know what happens when pigs fly - the price of bacon goes up!

Andrea Wetton (11)
Hardenhuish School, Wiltshire

A Day In The Life Of A Shoe Fitter In Clarks

It's freezing outside, I'm on the bus at the moment. It's 8 o'clock in the morning and I'm nearly there - at Clarks I mean, the place I work. I'm getting off now. I could swear my feet have turned into ice cubes.

I'm approaching the shop, going in the door and there's Sally, the girl I work with. We say hellos and drag our feet into the storeroom to sort out the boxes. This takes ages because there had been a new delivery early this morning. We have to stack them and put them in order of size and sort them all out, boring!

It's now 9 o'clock and the first customer has just arrived. By the way I work in the children's department, most of the time, anyway!

It's Saturday morning and this lady wants a pair of little boots for her two-year-old daughter. Normally it's fitting and finding the shoe that fits which takes the time up, but with this particular customer it was the shape and style, now this two-year-old couldn't care less, I wish it had been the same for the mother! The shoes have got to be pink, *and* the right shade, with a small amount of lilac, and first they had to be lace-ups. Then she changed her mind to buckles, then to velcro and back to buckles, they eventually left with the shoes about an hour later!

The next few customers are fine and get done quickly, but then a small lady came in with her nine-year-old brat! This girl got into a strop and kicked off one pair of shoes, which whacked me on the shoulder! Believe me, I found it hard to keep calm and ended up by chewing my lips. It didn't help that this girl found it absolutely hilarious and her mum didn't even tell her off!

It's 1 o'clock so I'm going to take my lunchbreak, I think I'll pop along to the café up the road, they do gorgeous sandwiches.

Right now I'm sitting on a park bench with a chicken and mayonnaise sandwich, a bottle of Coke and a flapjack.

By the way I live in a small flat with my flatmate Ellie, in a small town just outside Bath. Oh well, back to work, I s'pose, because it's 2 o'clock.

Steph, who works in the adult's department, went home ill, so I've got to cover for her. I sold loads of shoes, I counted about ten pairs! But one lady did buy three of those! I think I'm going to transfer to the adult's department, everything goes so much smoother! It's 5 o'clock now and eventually I'm going home - I'm whacked, but at least I don't have to do it all again until Monday!

Elizabeth Pullin (13)
Hardenhuish School, Wiltshire

A Night Of Mystery At Hargoyle Manor

It was a cold winter's night at Hargoyle Manor. Jane and Mary were playing Ludo in the Assembly Room when they heard a noise from their bedroom. It was an eerie creaking sound. They got up and walked along the hall towards their bedroom to investigate the sound. Jane turned the knob on the huge, carved wooden door very slowly as she knew it creaked dreadfully. They tiptoed in, Mary first, missing the squeaky floorboard, to the dark room. there was a loud bang then.
'Argh!'

* * * *

'We're afraid we have no leads ma'am.'
'You have no idea about anything?'
'No, the door was locked.'
'Couldn't they have locked it on the way out, or climbed out the window?'
'No, the key was on the inside of the door and the windows have been welded closed for many years now.'
'Do you have any fingerprints?'
'We're not sure, the forensic team are there now.'
'Well thank you.'

Chaz Sartain (12)
Hardenhuish School, Wiltshire

KING DUNCAN FOUND DEAD

King Duncan was found dead last night in Macbeth's castle. They were celebrating the battle against Norway where Scotland was victorious.

The guards were found dead outside Duncan's bedroom where he was sleeping They had blood on their cheeks and the daggers on their bodies.

Macbeth told our reporter that he had killed the two guards because he was so angry, he thought that the guards had killed Duncan.

Malcolm and Donalbain left under suspicious circumstances, it is rumoured that they've gone to England and Ireland.

Reporter
Jamie Bessell

Jamie Bessell (14)
Kingsdon Manor School, Somerset

THE HUNCHBACK OF NOTRE DAME

One rainy night, a young baby was abandoned on the steps of the Notre-Dame Cathedral and was found by an evil man named Frollo. Frollo was planning to kill the baby, but the Dean of the cathedral said, 'Don't! That is one life ruined, don't ruin another.'
So Frollo kept the baby and brought him up until he was a young man and kept him as the bellringer of Notre Dame. But because he rang the bells of the cathedral, he'd damaged his hearing and was becoming very deaf.

One sunny day, a new knight named Phoebus who was now working for Frollo, was walking down the street, when he came across a gypsy girl called Esmeralda, who was dancing to some music. Phoebus threw the gypsy girl some gold coins. She said, 'Thanks!' but she didn't mean it because Phoebus was a new soldier for Frollo and some of Frollo's guards came along and tried to capture Esmeralda, but she did some magic and disappeared.

Up in the bell tower, Quasimodo wondered what it would be like in the outside world. He was talking to his three friends, the gargoyles who were always trying to persuade him to get out of the bell tower but Quasimodo was scared that Frollo might catch him.
Then he was just going to leave when Frollo turned up and he said, 'I hope you weren't trying to escape.'
Quasimodo replied, 'No master!'

They sat down for lunch and Frollo said to Quasimodo, 'What is the ABC? What does A stand for?'
'Abomination Sir, B - blasphemy, C - contrition , D - damnation, E - eternal damnation and F - festival. No, no, sorry master!'

The next day the Festival of Fools began and Quasimodo went. He was having fun until the judging for the ugliest fool. The judges went through all the other men, they tried to pull Quasimodo's mask off, but it turned out to be his real face. He was still crowned the fool and then he felt happy, one man started bullying him and then others followed and he felt bad again but the gypsy girl saved him and they ran away.

They returned to the cathedral and Quasimodo was locked up with chains and they said there would be a bonfire in the town the following day and the gypsy girl would be burned at the stake.

Quasimodo gave up but the gargoyles persuaded him and he saved Esmeralda. They went back to the cathedral where they claimed sanctuary and stayed for hours.

Then the battle started. Quasimodo and Esmeralda were sitting down eating, when shots were fired at them, so Quasimodo escaped and left Esmeralda. He went and got all Esmeralda's gypsy friends who fought against the Kings' men. Quasimodo went back to the cathedral to get Esmeralda and he stayed with her. Then they went up to the roof and dropped a load of hot lava down, which killed most of Frollo's army; but they didn't kill Frollo, he escaped into the cathedral and Quasimodo and Frollo fought each other. Finally Quasimodo threw him off the top of the cathedral.

Phoebus and Esmeralda fell in love and Quasimodo didn't mind.

Ashley Mullen (12)
Kingsdon Manor School, Somerset

A Day In The Life Of A Pessimist

The train is dark; the air, a thick mist of tobacco smoke. Dust and cobwebs crawl the walls of the empty carriage. I cough violently as the stale air overwhelms me; the stench of failure fills the train. A charging shoulder strikes me like a herd of buffalo in a rush for the seat. I stand rather than endure a confrontation, recalling conversations I'd rather forget.

The train howls like a thousand tortured souls as it powers its way through the black, winding tunnel. I physically shudder until the howls are no more. I stand, looking pasty as I hear the clattering sound of the steel wheels negotiating the track.

The conductor approaches asking for my ticket. I start to *panic,* my heart is racing as I rummage through my pockets. A droplet of sweat runs down my forehead; I flinch as I prick my finger on a safety pin situated at the bottom of my left pocket. Finally, I grasp my ticket and present it to him. A fine speckle of blood from my finger drops on to the ticket. The conductor stares at me coldly, his face, a wrinkled, tired, grey complexion. I look away, avoiding his gaze; to stare would be rude. The conductor manoeuvres his way to the next compartment, his movement mirroring that of a penguin. My head sinks into my chest as I wait impatiently for my stop.

Observing the station, I notice boarded-up windows and degrading, juvenile graffiti. Pigeons have left their distinctive mark on the architecture. An unjust tribute to its Tudor craftsmanship and a sign of financial neglect to yet another public service.

I clench my bag hard with one hand, with the other I secure my hat against the bitter October winds. I start to struggle through the sea of people. A cacophony of conversation echoes around the station. Frantic commuters fight their way through the masses, like snakes slithering through the undergrowth. Their urgency unsettles me as they bob and weave toward the dull platform.

The overflowing fast food waste from mesh dustbins is a tale of our waning lifestyle. I shun the customers of the American-style food chain as I continue my battle through the throng. I stop at the gates and pick up a newspaper. The headline reads 'Sixth Victim Found'. I roll the paper and place it coolly in my luggage bag, having paid the newspaper vendor. Exchanging nods with the vendor, I stride through the gates.

I stare at the old oak tree, a few leaves remain. The leaves left are a beautiful rusty colour with a burning red tinge.

I holler for a taxi; a black cab appears as if by magic. I start to open the door and then a peculiar feeling runs through my body, the effects leave me shaken and disturbed. I take a while to gather myself and the sensation leaves me feeling nauseated.

A young lady with a pram approaches me to see if everything is fine. Without responding I clamber into the cab and close the door.

The roller coaster that foreshadows, has only just reached its infancy.

Sam Stephens (15)
Lockleaze School, Bristol

A Mouse In A Science Lab

A blurred vision like a painting disturbed by water: colours merging together, creating faces I didn't recognise in a room I'd never been in before. A soothing voice called me in the distance, but it was becoming fainter as my sight became clearer.

I was lying in a hospital bed; tubes and wires jammed into me like I was some kind of experiment: a mouse in a science lab.

What was I doing here? I tried to recall one thought, one memory, but . . . nothing. Questions tumbled over each other inside my head, searching for answers that weren't there. Simple things that people don't give a second thought. Family? Friends? Even my name: who was I? It was as if someone had thrown a brick through my past, shattering it into splinters of glass too small for me to see.

Suddenly the numbness I felt was replaced by blinding pain. Something was gripping my head like a vice, slowly increasing the pressure on my brain. My skin felt on fire . . .

Fire. At that thought a scene flickered before me. A group of teenagers. An aerosol can. A lighter. It was like an electric current had connected inside my head, causing sparks of long forgotten memories dancing through my mind. A dare. A fire. Screaming. Terrified faces running . . . away. Leaving me to burn so as to save their own backs.

The room slowly spun into a stormy darkness. The soothing voice was back, but this time I was close enough to reach it.

Katherine Bannon (13)
Maricourt RC High School, Liverpool

A Friendly Ghost

'I don't want to live in this house,' said Luke.
'Why not?' asked his mother. She was house-hunting and felt tired and cross.
'Because it hasn't got a ghost in it.'
Luke's mother stared at him. 'You don't want to live in this house because it hasn't got a ghost in it?' she asked.
'That's right. I like ghosts. In fact I need them for something important.'
Luke's mother was about to argue but she knew how obstinate her son could be and there were two more houses on the list.

The next house was gloomy and dark with a yew tree in the garden. This time Luke wouldn't even go in. 'There's no ghost in this house either,' he said, 'I promise you.'

The last house was modern, light and airy with big window.
'This one's alright,' said Luke. 'I like it.'
'Oh you do, do you?' said Luke's mother. 'I suppose this house has got a ghost in it?'
Luke nodded, 'Look!' he said, and pointed to the fireplace.
His mother looked - put her hand to her mouth - and screamed! 'Oh, my god Luke - why didn't you tell me?'
Luke shrugged, he'd seen the ghost immediately, a boy about his own age; he just assumed his mum had also.

Luke's mum walked up to the fireplace; inlaid over the mantle was a huge wrought iron mirror. His mum touched it. Luke gasped, she put her hand right through the boy - Luke and 'ghost' looked down at the hand, up at each other and back down at the hand.
'Luke, really, I look awful, why didn't you tell me my hair had gone frizzy? And look at the sight of me! Weight Watchers here I come . . .'
Luke's mother prattled on and on and on. Luke stood in amazement; obviously his mum was oblivious of 'ghost'.

Luke finally realised she'd stopped talking; he also realised she'd asked a question and was expecting a reply and judging by her expression the wrong answer could have extremely dire consequences for him. Luke, a leading light in the get-out-of-homework society at school, decided to sidestep. 'But Mum,' he ventured, 'I think you look lovely, and besides, think how much at home you must feel here to start talking about personal things. You didn't even see the ghost!'

Luke's mum sighed. Loudly. The house *was* perfect. Just the right size; newish, so only redecorating to do really; and much nearer school and work, cutting travelling time right down for both of them. Even better if Luke thought it had a ghost; he could carry on with his secret masterplan. 'Ghost Luke?' she said aloud looking around, flailing her arms in and out of the spectre's ectoplasm. 'Ghost' and Luke grinned. 'What do you think Luke? We can afford it now we've sold ours and the money has finally come through from grandma's house; I'm going to make an offer.'
Luke tried to look cool, 'Yeah, okay and there *is* a ghost - it's just what I'm looking for.'

During the next six frantic weeks Luke enhanced his great plan. When removal Saturday arrived it was also half-term and Luke couldn't wait to set up his computer in his room - a whole week of ghost games - he just felt in his heart that the spectral occupant of the house would be up for *'it'* too.

Luke didn't have long to wait. After supper - a take out - Mum and Aunt Claire opened a bottle of wine or three to toast the new house - pretty soon they were both 'toasted' as well. So Luke feigned tiredness and took to his room. When he opened the door 'ghost' was there, waiting. 'I knew you'd be here,' Luke smiled, 'but, who are you and how did you come to be here?'
The spirit sighed dramatically, 'You know Luke, ghosts aren't what people imagine them to be, we aren't just the 'restless soul of the unhappy dead, I, for one, am very happy.'
Luke nodded, 'Do you have a name?' he asked finally.
'Gavin,' came the reply.
'Really?' asked Luke excitedly, 'that's my middle name.'
Gavin nodded, 'I know,' he said. 'I also know your plans Luke; I can't wait.'

Luke said nothing: he didn't know what to say actually. He wondered all sorts, how had Gavin become a ghost, when, (no one had died in the house Luke had discovered, nor had the previous, and first occupants, had a son, teenage or otherwise,) and how did he know about the plan? After what seemed an age Gavin spoke. 'Come on then Luke, let's start this great adventure.'

They approached the computer together. Apart from the fact Gavin was see-through they were just like two modern boys, identical in cargo pants, T-shirts and trainers.

Luke logged on. IT was his speciality; a bit of a loner, he'd spent hours designing games and exploring the net, desperate to evaluate his great plan. He turned to look at Gavin. 'Are you ready?' he whispered almost inaudibly. In reply Gavin leapt forward and vanished into the screen. For a brief moment Luke felt a pain in his chest but he shrugged it off and began. The screen was alive with action, dragons, knights, warrior, kings, giants, ogres and the hero, Gavin, battled each other to rule the computer world.

Later Luke, exhausted, fell into a restless sleep, still pursuing the three-headed dragon he tossed and turned. Gavin had not re-materialised and Luke was concerned.

The next morning Luke's mum knocked at his door. Hearing no reply she opened it and went in, carrying a cup of tea and his computer magazine.

All was still. Too still. Too quiet. His mum flung open the curtains and turned to see Luke, deathly white on top of his bed, clutching a disk, in his cold, lifeless hand.

They told her it was 'one of those things' a heart attack. He was 15 for god's sake!

Some months later she finally had the courage to play the disk. Now she's hooked. She spends all her time with Luke Gavin Greatlock battling giants, dragons and ogres. Her son and his soul do battle together - forever!

Judith Clark (14)
Moorland School, Lancashire

ON A DARK NIGHT...

On the black and thundery night of January 15th she sat alone, curled up on the saggy sofa. Tears shone brightly in her eyes like early morning dew on delicate cobwebs. The film finished and the credits rolled. She hit the eject button and slowly got to her feet. She sighed and crept into the shadowy kitchen fumbling for the light switch. Her hand was lost in the dark hole and after a time she gave up. Exasperated she found a candle and struck a match, it flickered in the icy breeze and blew out. She lit another and another and eventually lit a candle. Its soft light gave out an angry glare.

Going out into the frosty hall she went slowly up the stairs. Her long hair drifting around her face: she was an angel.

In her room she set the candle on the dusty, empty shelf. A sudden draught blew out the candle at the same time as a bolt of lightning lit up the room.

There was a rapid thump at the door. She jumped. The thumping came again as she ran down the dusty stairs before stopping at the old wooden door. She opened the door a crack. A tall man loomed up out of the darkness. She saw his saturated hair and looked up into his ashen face. He pushed open the door and walked in. She smelt the tobacco and alcohol vapours on his breath.

He turned to her, his ghostly face glowing in the darkness. Her scream was drowned out by the peal of thunder. The lightning flashed and the lashing rain fell. It was then that she realised it was no good screaming.

Jo Cribb (15)
Norton Hill School, NE Somerset

A Day In The Life Of An Ant

My typical day might go like this:

Mounds of crumbled earth lie around me. I stare lazily at a tuft of grass protruding out the soggy earth. Beads of dew roll off the tip, their glassy surface reflecting the familiar wood, then smashing onto my shiny black back. I shake myself grumpily, opening my eyes. The trees look curved through my eyes' round lens. A smell of damp wood hangs in the air.

Suddenly - *crunch!* The grass is snapped and squashed with a scream only I can hear, leaving drops of watery mud over its previously vibrant, glossy green surface. Humans! A huge shaggy animal drags them along, its mouth gaping, tongue lolling, drooling and panting. Yellow-tinged spikes poke between its rubbery lips. It sends shivers down my segmented body. Why do humans stamp on us, and smash and scatter our complex homes? All those carefully made passages and corridors, buried. Just because we're small, it doesn't mean our feelings don't matter.

I scuttle off, searching for food. I disappear under a huge, waxy green leaf, then reappear with a jagged piece my teeth have sawn off. We're strong creatures you know. We can carry things much bigger than ourselves. All day, every day, carrying leaves to grow delicious mould on. I'm proud of my beautiful crops.

After that long day, naturally I'm tired, so I leave the rustling foliage and dying noise behind, and retreat to my neatly made bed chamber, taking each day as it comes.

Emma Pink (12)
Norton Hill School, NE Somerset

KIM

Have you ever had a secret so deep, so unusual, that one word of it would seal your very destruction? I have. And that is the reason I'm here writing this.

I guess from the very beginning I knew I was different from others, but if I'd known how different, I don't think I would have bothered being born. Even when I was a baby, whenever I wanted something, my mother would get a weird feeling up her spine, like someone had just dropped an ice cream down her neck.

My father has always been a mystery. I have never seen him, and I'm not allowed to speak of him. Oh, before I start, you'll probably need to know my name. It's Kim Jones. I'm a girl. I have black hair and bright green eyes. I hate dresses, and I'm twelve years old.

The ground had turned to marble with the frost. I enjoyed the happiness of walking home from school with my friends, Jess - the bossy one and Mark - the confident one. I let their chatting and chirping wash over me as we neared my house. I gestured farewell to my companions as I reached the gate.

Upon entering the kitchen, I knew something was wrong. I could smell it in the air - fear. My mum rushed into the room, looking like death had come knocking on the door. In her hand she clutched the phone like it was a bomb.

Somebody pounded on the door. 'Let us in, Mrs Jones. We won't hurt you if you just give up the kid.'

White sparks flashed from my eyes, a tell-tale sign that I was getting scared. Mum saw it and knew I was going to cause trouble. She picked up a bottle of something and a wet cloth. She ripped up some floorboards and held the cloth to my mouth. The bangs on the door were getting louder. I was getting drowsier. The damp cloth had made me strangely tired and unconnected to my body, which was at that moment being placed in the space under the floorboards.

Then I was covered up. The boards were being jammed hurriedly into place. Soon space for just one board was left. I stared half-heartedly into my mother's tear-streaked face one last time; then the last board - darkness. One word rang out in my mind. Sleep, sleep, sleep.

I came to, choking on smoke-filled air. Fire blazed furiously above me. Worse still, I was trapped. I clawed at anything and everything, not knowing anything in my oxygen-deprived mind, other than that I had to get out of this cramped torture chamber.

My eyes flamed with anger and fear. Suddenly I felt something erupt from within. In an explosion of lightning that came from deep inside me, the roof of my prison became a smouldering hole. I scrambled out of my almost grave and stumbled to the firmly shut door, which was blown across the street at my command.

After I breathed in clean, fresh air, I regained enough presence of mind to stagger to a nearby alleyway before I passed away into a comforting blanket of sleep.

A couple of days later, I discovered my mum had been found murdered, and everybody thought me dead too. I watched the funeral from a distance. I lurked in the shadows, then slid silently away to leave messages to my two best friends.

I hovered in the nearby woods at sundown to see if they would come, as I had wrote in the messages. They came. They walked up to me like they were dead themselves. After they had assured themselves that I was in fact real, I told them my story and my secret.

I have the supernatural power of electricity.
'What are you going to do now?' Mark whispered while Jess cut my scorched hair.
'I am going to leave, to see if there are others like me, more mutants, more gifts and more curses.' I had thought this through. 'I will find where I belong.'

And eventually I did, but that's another story.

Samantha Austin (15)
Norton Hill School, NE Somerset

AGAINST THE STORM

The rain slashed angrily against her face, stabbing at her like a thousand needles. Overhead thunder rolled dominantly aloft in the black night sky, ploughing through the air, swallowing all that it came across. Wind erased anything that was unlucky enough to fall in its path, clinging on to it with a God-like grip and refusing to let go.

Yet still she carried on, the rain stinging her bare red arms like glass bullets that shatter after making contact. Her vision was blurred; she could just make out the soaring trees that loomed above her head, blowing recklessly in the display of natural fury. Thunder pounced persistently about her, getting louder and louder, surrounding her in a blanket of continuous commotion. The wind whipped uncaringly around her head; twisting her dark curly hair in front of her colourless, ghost-like face.

Pale and shaking all over, she dragged her drenched, almost lifeless body another step forward. Further on into the grim, insensitive atmosphere that lay ahead. Stumbling over uneven ground, heart pounding against her rib cage, she tried to clear her buzzing head and work out what to do. For the first time she was fully aware of just how alone she was.

After what seemed like forever, but could only have been minutes, she continued to haul herself forward, every movement causing her pain. Determined and ready to face whatever was thrown at her she plodded on, her giant green eyes shining brightly through the sheets of torrential rain.

Olivia McGlone (15)
Norton Hill School, NE Somerset

DREAMS

Listening to the rapturous welcome that sang out from the people his heart swelled inside his chest to such a size that it almost entirely quashed the nervous movements of his stomach. For a moment his mind levitated to a plane on which he was equalled by all, but still at the foot of God.

He took the first few steps to his podium and looked out at the sea of colour that stretched before him, causing his eyes to glisten with thankful tears. All around cheers and praise rang out like hymns and in his presence some were so overcome they dropped to their knees. Announcing his first words brought a stillness of true intent listening from the droves that took his word as prayer and practised what he preached.

His dream was for the black and white screen to die and for everyone to see the many interesting and dynamic colours of the world.

The atmosphere, potent with excitement and anticipation of his every word, brought life to every single person who stood in the presence of Lincoln's Memorial and inspired hope into their souls. As he concluded his deliverance the congregation cheered with joy at his presence.

Even once his body was no longer there and his heart was no longer swelling and pumping, owing to one of the coldest bullets that ever existed, his presence would always be remembered and millions give thanks at the sound of the name of Martin Luther King Junior.

Emma Wilding (16)
Penwortham Girls' High School, North Somerset

IT'S ALL MY FAULT

I don't really know what's happened, and I don't want to know. I'm just lying in the hospital waiting for someone to notice me. I try to speak but the words won't come out, I try so hard but no one listens, I shout for help but I can't breathe. I lose hope, 'Help me, help m . . .'

'Help,' cried the nurse as the heart monitor started to bleep. 'She's unconscious.'
Twelve other paramedics ran to help with the crash team and started operating, 15 chest compressions, 10 mouth-to-mouth resuscitations.
'She's still failing.'
'Don't lose hope, carry on.'
They repeated this operation twice more, eventually Mary-Jane regained consciousness and was able to breathe.
Mary-Jane's parents rushed into the ward to console her.
'Mary, what's happened?' cried Mary's mother as she waited for her daughter to reply. She didn't, she couldn't speak.
'Hello Mr and Mrs Griswold,' sighed the doctor, 'may I have a word?' The doctor, a police inspector, Mr and Mrs Griswold stepped into his office. 'It appears that Mary-Jane and her friend Emily were setting fire to bins and then some boys, or a gang of boys, came up and beat Mary up and left her to die, until someone phoned us. Mary-Jane knew them, they were arguing with them and she accidentally pushed Emily into the fire. She's dead! I'm sorry but Mary-Jane might not live that long either. She can't talk, it's that bad.'

Lauri Smith (12)
Penwortham Girls' High School, North Somerset

My Day In The Life Of A Dolphin Which Then Turned Into A Disaster!

I woke up and felt all wet like I had been in the bath for ages and gone all wrinkly. Then I opened my eyes and I was in the sea and was a dolphin. Wow! A dolphin! I had always wanted to swim with dolphins ever since I was little and now I could.

I couldn't talk like I normally did. I just made noises like singing to other people. I was swimming along but then I felt something behind me. I turned around and it was a *shark* . . . my worst nightmare. Well what could I do except swim - and fast! It was coming closer and closer to me. Then, somehow, I lost it - thank goodness. A boat had come along and the shark went for the boat instead.

Then I found myself back in my own bed and everything was safe again. And then Mum called me for breakfast. What an adventure I'd had!

Amy Cabble (12)
Priory Community School, North Somerset

THE DARE

I never meant it to go this far. It started as a harmless dare. It was only Cloanfield Manor after all. Easy, no problem.

As I approached the house, there was an unsettled, tense atmosphere. I felt so alone, yet I knew I wasn't. I clambered onto the porch being as cautious as a mother with kittens. The place was derelict and the windows were boarded. Moss was creeping up the walls. An old spindly tree dominated the garden.

My hands were trembling as I grabbed the rusted door handle and slowly twisted it. Before I knew it I was inside. The floorboards were creaking and rubble was scattered everywhere. I gazed around; I had never felt like this before. The bitter coldness belted me. From the dim light I thought I saw something trickling down the wall. From the corner of my eye I could have sworn I saw a shadow drift past. I tried to convince myself it was just my imagination, I had this horrible feeling it wasn't.

From out of nowhere an organ began to play an empty, depressing tune. Laughter filled the room. A ghostly whisper floated past me. A cold shiver ran down my spine. I had to get out.

With my legs dragging behind me I ran to the door and shook the handle as hard as I could. I had never been so happy to be outside. I ran for miles and never looked back.

Kirsty Holburd (13)
Priory Community School, North Somerset

THE WOLVINES

Suddenly my big brother and I saw a lovely, angelic-looking creature eating the grass.

'Let's go and touch it,' Paul said excitedly.

Just as he was about to touch it, my brother and I found ourselves surrounded by these strange things. They seemed angry. I said to Paul that maybe they were hungry.

Paul let out a great scream. *'Run!'* he bellowed, *'run!'*

The creatures began to gain on us but somehow we kept on running and we began to lose them. Just as it looked as though we would escape, Paul fell over and hurt his leg and he could not move. 'Go! Before they get you! he yelled at me.

I charged off but as I looked back, my brother had gone.

I still don't forgive myself for what happened. It was six years ago and I will never forget.

Jamie Rosser (12)
Priory Community School, North Somerset

THE BREATHING

I sat in the corner, cold, scared, shivering, a frozen breeze brushed past my face. I didn't want to move, I heard the noise again. It sounded like nails scratching a chalkboard.

I was sat in the corner of the old ruined school, I had run away from home, this was the last place anyone would look because it was meant to be haunted. I now believe that it was.

It was pitch-black, the only light was coming from the full moon outside. The noise had stopped the second my phone had started to ring. I didn't know the number but I still answered. A cold whisper rang in my ear. The voice said, 'Run.' But then it started the breathing, it sounded like I do when I have just ran.

Wherever the noise was coming from it was in this room. I froze, the classroom light started to flash on and off, on and off. Then there was a bang like something had dropped a TV, but the light stopped flickering and the room was illuminated.

I looked around to see what it was. I saw huge jaws with razor-sharp teeth, then I heard a manly voice shout, *'Heel,'* and what I thought was a monster walked away and there stood a policeman, they had found me! *I'm in so much trouble,* was all I could think about.

Emma Douglas (13)
Priory Community School, North Somerset

Day 126

I'm still alive. I don't know how. There are seven people left in my regiment: me, Sarge, Corporal Steve, John, Chris, Tom and the only girl left, Crystal. We never thought that the war would go on for this long when we signed up. I saw my mate James die today. He stood up to stretch and got shot in the head four times, but the thing that bothers me is that we can't give them a proper funeral. They're making an awful smell and bringing rats and flies. Two people have already died from the disease that the rats and flies carry.

The enemy is closing in fast but we are slowly taking them out every night. The enemy started off with well over 100,000 soldiers and we have only had 50,000, but we have got them down to about 20,000. We have only got about 5,000 left, so it is going to be a tough battle but if we try our best we can do it. The only problem is that most of us do not have any energy to fight because there's no food left and we cannot sleep.

I will write tomorrow - if I am still alive.

Ali O'Brien (12)
Priory Community School, North Somerset

The Haunted Mansion

I ran to the door desperately shaking it but it would not open. I stood there for what seemed an eternity. I heard a knock. The knock got louder until it was a bang. I slowly walked backwards into a dark corner.

The door swung open. Lightning flashed to reveal a dark figure. Its yellow eyes gleamed in the dark. It wore long black robes and was really tall. It walked in and locked the door behind it. It slowly walked towards the stairs. I followed.

It went into a dark room lighting candles, as it did this it was chanting something but I could not understand what it was saying. As the candle brightened, I saw a dead body which I believed was a human sacrifice. It drank the body's blood.

Once it had finished it walked over to the window, looking at the full moon. I walked in and tripped on an unsteady floorboard. The creature reacted and turned around. It now had blood dripping from its teeth.

I crawled backwards only to bump into the dead body, the creature walked towards me. I was scared. The creature was close when I caught sight of a knife next to me which had been used for the sacrifice.

I grabbed the knife and stumbled as the creature struck me across the face, so I stabbed it in the heart. It cried in agony and fell to the floor. Suddenly the doors opened. Without hesitation I ran downstairs and through the front door, I looked back to see a ghostly head come out the front door screaming. It chased me across the field. I ran and did not look back until I got home.

Luke Patrick (12)
Priory Community School, North Somerset

LOCH NESS MONSTER

The excitement I felt in the car as we left for our holiday was overwhelming. My heart was beating faster, especially when we started to see mountains.

As we reached our hotel I saw the loch on the left. The hotel was right on the edge of the loch with views of the surrounding mountains, with their peaks shielded in a mist.

When we got into the hotel we could hear the sound of bagpipes playing. A man in a tartan hat showed us to our room. It had a four-poster bed which had tartan curtains around it. The windows were big and we had a good view of the loch. My parents and I went down to the loch. There was a mist on the water, it made it difficult to see, then I saw something. The mist cleared and I saw the monster. It had a small head, long nose and a long neck. It was Nessie, she was beautiful. Slowly, she disappeared back into the water, the mist rolled in again.

We went back to the hotel and changed for dinner. The food was lovely. We had steak and chips for main course and for sweet we had bananas stuffed with strawberry and chocolate ice cream with chocolate sauce over the top. The best bit about the evening was talking about what we had seen, the views, the hills, the water on the loch, the mist and - best of all - seeing the Loch Ness monster and being with my family.

Caroline Quick (14)
Priory Community School, North Somerset

DAVID'S DISASTROUS DAY - DIARY ENTRY

Oh my god, I have had the most terrifying day and it all started like this:

I was planning to get up as usual. Go to training, play the big game, England Vs France, but it did not turn out like that.

Seven o'clock my alarm went off with Victoria singing, 'I'll tell you what I want what I really really want.' I thought to myself, oh no what? What does Victoria really want today? Brooklyn came in with Victoria behind him singing happy birthday to me.

I got to work at about ten and got ready to play. I was so nervous about playing the game on my birthday. It was live on TV and I was captain.

No one said happy birthday to me, not even my best mate Michael Owen. So I just went along with it, but I felt upset.

We got outside on the pitch and I looked up at the big TV screen. It was filled with my face. All the teams and fans started singing happy birthday and cheering.
Michael came and said, 'Didn't think I'd forgotten did you?' and he gave me a pair of golden slippers, the ones I have wanted for ages, to play the big game. I put them on and played.

Michael had missed two penalties; I got so angry in the changing rooms I threw a slipper at him. It went right in his eye and he was rushed to hospital. He cannot play football for two weeks now. What a day!

Harriet Glimstead (13)
Priory Community School, North Somerset

MY STORY!

The coldness of the shore here in my hometown makes everything come back. I don't care - not anymore. I have lost every possession close to me. I have nothing left. My memory is long, very long, especially as I was so young when all this happened.

My parents Liz and John were the nicest people possible. Now they have gone. Their life just slipped away.

One day I was in my back garden at my house. My dad at work, my mother inside packing. Father worked as a bank manager - very high-classed.

On this particularly gloomy day, Father came back from work early. Shouting at Mother it was clear he was drunk. I had never seen him like this. He had lost his job, come home and taken it all out on Mother. I overheard Father saying we were going to his boat that he had bought six months before.

We got to the harbour quickly as it was only a five minute drive, and loaded all our stuff onto the boat. As we'd left the house, we had walked out to find a for sale sign in the front garden. Father leaving his pride and joy of a home, things must have been bad.

We stepped onto the boat and I knew something was wrong. It was stepping onto a death trap. One mile out and the boat stopped. It was late at night, my mother came into my cabin and told me to wrap up warm and then I felt alone.

I stepped out and found I *was* alone.

Rachel Rowlands (13)
Priory Community School, North Somerset

THE DERELICT MANSION

I realised that I'd been standing on the same spot for at least 20 minutes and decided that I couldn't hang around any longer. I took a step towards the staircase. As I came nearer to the top of the stairs my eyes focused on an old door. It looked as if it had been hand carved, just looking at it you could see how long it would have taken to make. You could see every little detail. Then, out of the corner of my eye, I saw another door. I crept over to it and placed my hand on the doorknob, a shiver went right through me. I turned the handle.

This time it was open. I walked through and hid myself in the corner. Scanning the room I found nothing, but I heard a scattering sound. It's a mouse, I thought to myself. The air was damp and cold and I could smell dust. I wished I was anywhere but there.

Suddenly, from the landing, I heard a banging sound. Faster and faster it came. I ran and ran until I finally gave up and broke down onto the hard wooden boards.

By this time the banging sound had gone. I managed to pull myself up and found myself in a long corridor with blood on the walls. Which way should I go?

Then a gigantic figure loomed over me and tapped me on the shoulder. 'Argh!' I cried as a knife headed towards me . . .

Sam Stitson (12)
Priory Community School, North Somerset

VOICES

Then I heard it. The laughter of two children filled the room above. I picked up one of the flickering candles and walked steadily and cautiously towards the wall. The children's laughter turned to screaming. Stood like a statue, I didn't know what to do. The candle glowed brightly as I looked at the wall. Blood. Trickling down. Right down to the bottom. Walking towards the door, the candle blew out. Silence reigned. I opened the door and walked out, a flight of stairs in front of me. I walked up them very slowly and warily.

A long corridor with four doors awaited me. I went to the first one, pushed it open and there it was . . . the most intricately decorated silver box that I have ever seen in my life. It was slap bang in the middle of the room; a funny buzzing noise was beginning to emanate from the box. But that wasn't the only thing in there.

There was a painting that filled the whole side of a wall. It was a family - a mother, a father and two children. As I looked closely I could see that something was wrong with them. Their features were being rubbed away. The mother looked at me as if she was pleading with me to help them, but what could I do? What did she want? And then I remembered the children's laughter . . .

Kerry Knight (13)
Priory Community School, North Somerset

THE BILLABONG GAMES

April 2nd 2003 the Billabong Games opening day and Tony Hawk is the first man up. He drops in 23 foot vert up the other side and does a del mar indy, comes back down, comes out the half-pipe up the spine and a-a-a sol-flip! Oh no, he's bailed! That's his go over.

Her comes Eric Koston, drops in up the pipe, fingerflip trick . . . just lands it up, *backflip 180!* Up it again, 180 melon. Can he get 720? No! He's bailed, that's him finished.

Matt Hoffman on his BMX in a fat suit is next. He attempts to drop in . . . ooohhh! He has got to have broken his leg.

(On the tannoy) 'Ladies and gentlemen, it's confirmed that Matt Hoffman has a broken leg.'

(Three hours later) 'Matt Hoffman has had to have his leg amputated because two bones in his leg have been destroyed. His kneecap was non-existent.

On a better note Tony Hawk has won the Billabong Games with the 900%. Eric Koston came second with a 540 big spin.

Well, Jim, that was a brilliant games. I wonder if next year's will be any better?'

Craig Davies (13)
Priory Community School, North Somerset

GALYUS AND THE DRAGON

250 years ago, to this day, a boy called Galyus saved a king and his country, and this is how it goes . . .

'Dad, Dad,' yelled Galyus.
'What is it my son?' replied Sir James.
'Street people are talking about a dragon in the caves,' when Galyus said this he said it quietly as he did not want to embarrass his father.
'Guards, go to the caves!' shouted the king.

As the guards ran out to the caves they armed themselves with swords and shields. They ran out to the caves to see if what Galyus and the street people said was true. They could see nothing. The caves smelt like burning fire. All of a sudden an almighty roar sounded out. *Crunch!* the guards were no more.

'It's been too long, I'm going Father. See you later,' said Galyus.
'Wait son I will give you the best sword and shield ever made.'
Twenty minutes later Galyus set off to the caves.

As he slowly entered the caves he could hear a crunching sound, as he got deeper into the caves the crunching got louder. There it was - as he turned the corner he saw it, the dragon eating. But the dragon did not see him. He slowly pulled out his sword, ran up to the dragon and pushed the sword through the monster's throat. He turned to go home, but as he turned, Galyus found he now faced a whole army of dragons.

Matthew Tucker (12)
Priory Community School, North Somerset

REVENGE

Revenge in his eyes was coming closer to fruition. The void in his heart was craving for retribution.

He breathed heavily as he edged closer and closer to his destination. Every step he made, he knew he was getting angrier and angrier, and more frustrated. Knowing what Darren had done, how he had betrayed his trust, how he'd stabbed him in the back and left him to suffer in a rotten police cell.

That was why he was here now, craving revenge - and out to get it. He had gone to prison after being set up by Darren. He had been in his house watching television when he heard a shot. Someone had been dumped in his shed and *his* hair was scattered all over the dead man's body.

Darren had been his alibi for goodness sake.

He arrived outside Darren's house with his trustworthy cell mate's bladed knife in his hand. Going round the back of the house, he opened the door, cautiously walked inside and tiptoed behind Darren's sofa. He raised his knife and plunged it into the back of Darren's head and, with a sickening crunch, Darren fell to the floor. *He* had lost everything that night he was framed, his wife, job and money.

DCI Blaisdon fled into the night and was never seen again.

Jasmine Harrison (13)
Priory Community School, North Somerset

A Day In The Life Of . . . A Cartoon Character

My day starts at . . . well . . . it's really up to the cartoonists to decide. Basically, at that time, I'm just a plain piece of white paper. Anyway, when the cartoonists do start sketching me, they do it softly and calmly. However, soon they become frustrated and begin to frantically rub me out. (Making me go all furry whilst doing so.)

Eventually, they declare that I look perfect, (well of course I do!) and they begin the painful process of going over me, darker and harder. I think that what they're really doing is relieving their stress. It's agony - as if I'm being tattooed all over. Once this extremely painful experience is over, I'm actually a full cartoon character, except I'm black and white.

This is the point when the cartoonists go away and 'discuss' (argue) about the colours to use. (Leaving me standing there on the paper with my legs aching badly). Eventually they come to a decision and get on with the colour process. This part tickles. Although, it really stings when they do my eyes (but they don't respect my feelings - how dare they!) Once I'm completely coloured I'm ready for my starring role in . . . 'Superfluff the Dustball!'

In this I'm a handsome ball of dust who saves the world and who everybody loves. But, as you can probably guess, saving the world is a pretty tiring job. So, once the world's safe, I get taken to my dressing room (aka a drawer) and get my shut-eye. Goodnight.

Amy Coppack (13)
Priory Community School, North Somerset

A Day In The Life Of A Schoolgirl's Pen!

I come to school in the morning, waiting to be assigned to my first task. I am a golden fountain pen and I live in a gloomy case with the other common stationery. My blue runny blood helps create my master's work. I can write cunning notes full of secrets and gossip, clever, witty essays that always gain top marks and even draw the odd doodle or two!

I look at the lonely pencil sharpenings, oh what it must be to be discarded in that way. The plain pencils in their packs being continually scraped of their pride. The colourful crayons, quite bright and brassy in their day, but now they lay half bent and broken like poor old soldiers of war. They will not be in use for much longer. I am lucky for this will never be *my* fate.

I hear the jolt of the zip and a hand reaches to me. I am called up for duty. My quick, yet fluent nib begins its intricate work. Then suddenly, mid paragraph, I begin to choke, what's happening to me? I am scratched roughly against the paper. I feel my blood run dry and I am not refilled.

'Can I borrow a pen?' I hear my master call.
'Sure,' a fellow voice replies.
I am thrown to the bottom of the case where I lay motionless, useless, forgotten.

So there I stay, abandoned. Living forever with the humiliation that I was replaced by a ball-point pen!

Jade Elizabeth Pickett (14)
Priory Community School, North Somerset

EVADING ARREST

In a school in the heart of Oxford, Ian whispered, 'It's too hot in here isn't it?'

'Yeah, stuffy too, if only we could get out, I can't stand Social Education,' sneezed Eddek.

'It will be lunch soon, how do you fancy skiving afterwards?'

'Yeah, go on then,' replied Eddek.

When the bell rang they made a quick exit and ran to the cinema. Psycho 2, the latest horror film, was showing. Both boys were too grown up to admit being frightened, but deep down they felt uneasy. Out in the daylight they went to the shops to calm themselves down.

In the music shop, Eddek said, 'I dare you to steal those CDs.'

'No,' replied Ian hastily.

'You're scared aren't you?'

Ian put them in his jacket and ran out of the shop.

In ten minutes their world changed. They had been caught on CCTV and two policemen were chasing them. The boys were quicker, but they didn't know the city as well. The police called for reinforcements who chased them on motorbikes. The friends were soon caught, pinned to the floor and arrested.

Later, in the police station, they were told that they could go to prison, this shocked them into a state of total silence. Now they both knew what it meant to be scared.

A week later they were in court charged with shoplifting and evading arrest. They were sentenced to ten weeks community service and fined five hundred pounds.

Ben Rogers (13)
Priory Community School, North Somerset

THE WOODEN SHOE

Rex stepped off the merry-go-round once again. *There isn't a lot to do here,* thought Rex. He had been at the fair for nearly an hour and had only found a merry-go-round and a helter-skelter. But his luck would change.

On his way out Rex noticed a strange tent. *That wasn't there before,* thought Rex, or at least he thought because soon after there was a voice. 'It wasn't,' said the mysterious voice. Rex nearly jumped out of his skin, but continued into the tent nonetheless.

On the other side there was a blinding light.
'Hello, man of dog's name!' boomed the voice, as it spoke the light brightened. Rex was about to reveal his anger about this statement, but thought better of it. 'Beware the wooden shoe!' said the voice, 'for there you shall meet your end!'

Whilst on his way home Rex began to think about his fate and what it could have to do with a wooden shoe. *How could he die from a wooden shoe?* Rex thought. He could trip on one at the top of some stairs or it could hit him in the head somehow. *I don't even own a pair of wooden shoes,* thought Rex.

He was so consumed in thought that he hadn't noticed where he was. He had walked onto a building site and was on the edge of a very deep hole. His last thought was, *the voice had to be wrong.*

Harvie Agnew (14)
Priory Community School, North Somerset

A Day In The Life Of A Cold-Blooded Assassin

I wake up, the blood and drink of the night before, still wavering on my mind. The shouts, the screams . . . the gunshots.

I make my way down the long, chandeliered corridor towards the bathroom. As I reach the basin, my intestines get the better of me and the remainder of my last night's binge spews forth from my foul-tongued mouth and my recent vindaloo curry gushes out, like blood taken by a single, deadly bullet. So much curry, so much vomit, so much blood . . .

I force my head away from the urinal and use what seems like my last ounce of strength to pull the flush before falling backwards on the stone-cold floor, feeling I would never rise again.

So many images that flashed before my eyes. Men, women, drink, smoke, cigars, guns, bullets, blood.

I pull myself up to the sink and pull down a jar of pills and force it open. I swallow two of them and welcome their disgusting, relieving taste. I stare down at my hands, before barely stopping myself from bringing my guts up again. The now dark blood of last night still lay upon my hands.

As I turn the tap and start to scrub viciously, I try to convince myself, 'A little water clears me of this deed.' I stared into the mirror and despised the heartless fiend I saw. A murderer and assassin.

I turned away from the 14-year-old female face I hated so much . . .

Alex Knapp (14)
Priory Community School, North Somerset

THE BEAST OF BAGOON

The sun rose up over the swamps of Bagoon, winding its way through the mist, casting a red hue over the fermenting plants.

Tansu was on the edge of the swamp. He wasn't a tall man and not very strong, but what he lacked in brawn he made up for in wit. He was taking his annual visit to his brother, Lansha. Normally there was no real danger in the form of animals, but Tansu had heard troubling stories of late. Some people believed in the 'Beast of Bagoon', and that it had been lying dormant, until now.

Tansu took a deep breath and calmly strode down the path. After a few hundred metres he found an old rune hanging from a tree in the middle of two tracks. It read: *To the right, there be dragons* and *To the left, you may walk safely*. The right path went over the swamp on a walkway; the left went around the edge and was three times as long. Tansu had always taken the right road and he saw no reason to stop now.

As he strutted along the creaky wooden planks silence was suddenly broken by birds skimming the water as they took flight. Tansu felt weakness in his foot and the plank snapped, sending him tumbling into the swamp. He struggled his way to the surface and gasped for air. The walkway was unreachable. There was a long, deep groan from under the water and it wasn't any normal animal.

Ben Harris (14)
Priory Community School, North Somerset

THE TRAVELLER

The lightning stabs the ferocious blue sky, the clouds cry out in pain as they bleed a monsoon of rain. The traveller sits on an empty box watching the dirt in the gutter being swept away by the miniature tsunamis surging every now and again.

He feels no coldness towards the people scurrying along the dark pavements, arm in arm with their loved ones.

The traveller had a wife, the traveller had a life, but all he has now is a coat, trousers and that blank, expressionless face, staring into the rain, willing it to stop.

Nobody usually looked at him, but when they did they were plunged into his past. Figures spun around them and they were lost in a frenzy of shouts and colours, moving so fast they merged into one another.

The traveller stares at the graffiti-soaked wall opposite and thinks of ways to keep dry on this winter night. He curls up underneath the box for it will be some sanctuary from the rain and he drifts off to sleep. He sleeps a long, heavy sleep with memories of his past, his childhood.

The night grows colder and eventually his breaths grow further apart until no steam rises from his bearded mouth. The clouds stop crying and no longer bleed as the traveller had willed them to do for so long.

The miniature tsunamis no longer swept away the dirt from the gutter. The traveller had died opposite the graffiti-soaked wall, but nobody will ever remember him.

Charlotte Warren (14)
Priory Community School, North Somerset

A Day In The Life Of A School Bully

8.30am when most people are already trapped at school, I wake up. I drag myself out of bed and grab food as I watch for him out of my window. By 9am I've got him, scared him and sit satisfied in Class 1.

Lessons are spent surrounded by lads walking the long way around the class and girls dishing out dirty looks, always directed at me.

Break time, bike sheds, smoking. I have a fag by myself then go to find my friends, Perry and Rob, but it takes me ages. When I do see them I call their names, but they never seem to hear me straight away. They finally see me and they seem happy to see me. They have excuses, but I don't care and this is when I wonder if they are really my mates or are just scared of me, but they're there for me so I don't care.

Lessons drag on the same as ever and lunch is the same as break except we find him - the kid from the morning - and once again scare the living daylights out of him.

3.30pm, go home and reflect on how the day went. I know what I do is wrong, but if my stepdad can get away with it, so can I. I try to dash upstairs, like the kid tries to dash past my house every morning, but I catch him, like he always catches me.

Kirstie Keir (14)
Priory Community School, North Somerset

A Day In The Life Of A Remote Control

I wake up to the crushing weight from the cushion above me. Then all the shouting of, 'Where are they? They were here last night.' Eventually they find me and manhandle me with very little care, then press my buttons endlessly.

As soon as the smaller people go to school, I'm left alone. At last, my part of the day off.

Midday has come, the big people are back, but not for long. I am only used now and again. The big people get this thing called food and shoot off. I am left to sleep for a whole three hours.

The time has come, little people are back from a place they call school (I've heard it's a crazy town where everyone is nasty). School gets the children so exasperated, which causes me to get hurled and abused. I end up in a different place every two minutes. The constant flicking from channel to channel really exhausts me. When the children try to hide me to stay on the channel that they want, I am always in a dark and smelly place.

Eventually the adults say, 'It's our television and we're watching what we want!' Only then do I get a rest, after they have chosen what they want.

I turn the television on to a movie channel, get tossed onto a cushion and the day ends, only to sleep in an awkward position until the new day starts. Oh, it's a hard life changing channels.

Joe Fisher (14)
Priory Community School, North Somerset

THE MARVELLOUS BEAST

Charles had tracked the yeti across many continents to the snow-painted mountains of the Himalayas. No creature that walks this Earth is more elusive than the yeti. The master of camouflage, the white beast, the abominable snowman are just a handful of the labels attached to the yeti. The yeti is not known to be good or bad.

Charles has dedicated his life to the pursuit of the creature, but up to now his lifetime had only provided brief glimpses. This time though there was a better chance to spot this magnificent beast, now we join Charles in the hunt for the yeti.

Charles stormed across the frozen lake knowing that a misplaced step would cause his untimely death. He carried on across the lake until he was to be stopped by a crack that rang out like a bell in the silence of a Sunday morning; he fell on to his hands and knees. He tried to crawl away to the side, but he was stopped by another crack. His death was inevitable until, two long white arms reached out from under the water to lift him off the ice. The arms had knocked him unconscious; Charles was re-living his whole life from his birth, to his first sighting of the marvellous beast, up to the present day of his death.

At that moment Charles regained consciousness surprised to find that he could still take a breath.

Oliver Hughes (14)
Priory Community School, North Somerset

REBELLION OF MIDNIGHT MEN

Tony looked up at the blazing office block, staring in a state of shock and disbelief, as in turn another office was cremated before him. As the last office began to ignite, cherry-coloured smoke emerged from the ground floor before pouring from the open upper floor windows, drifting into the shadow of the moonlit street.

With sirens pounding, the city awoke. In office number 306, Charlie Baker had been working late. Oblivious that he was there, the city moved on whilst his lifeless, limp body was engulfed in flames. The unconscious cries for help within the deceased Mr Baker, made no sound. Tony's heart pounded as his bitter mind reached reality. Deep inside his twisted head he adored the smell of burning. The offices where he worked, no longer remained.

Panic filled the night sky as people fled their homes. Others lay asleep unaware that their jobs drowned themselves in indescribable horror. This was not the first terrorist attack on the city and the fire department had been under remarkable pressure during the past month. The city's employees were understandably devastated as yet another building ablaze, glowed on through the night. Women cluttered the smoke-filled streets, babies terrified, weeping and miserable. News reporters screened their newest release, 'Pack small bags, take only essentials, be attentive, our city is on Red Alert!'

Emma Perks (14)
Priory Community School, North Somerset

A Day In The Life Of A Can!

Another day of gang warfare. A day of competition, aggression, pride and shame. Who will the people go for? It's up to us to make their decision.

Let me explain quickly: for 80 odd years now, from our great-grandparents' parents, there has been a battle of the brands. In total there are eight contenders, willing to risk all to become the greatest.

We live in the chiller room, where we freshen up and look pretty to the judges who come. Every morning begins with the frantic rush of make-up. Fights often break out as the stress is immense and all the teams are bundled in together and they bump into each other as they are on their way to get polished or something.

After the rush has finished, we all assume our positions and begin to look as eye-catching as possible. The lights on our house are turned on and we all secretly pray to be the one, or one of the ones who will be chosen. It's like Hell. The judges slot in the money, press their choice of the holy buttons. Heartbeats rise as the few, everlasting seconds slowly tick away, until one of us will fall and be grasped by the hand!

An outburst of cries fills the house, both joy and pain. The leader board is updated and the scores read out.

Anyway, I've got to go now and remember, vote for Coke!

Dan Slade (14)
Priory Community School, North Somerset

A Day In The Life Of A Packed Lunch

Well, I start my day in a loaf of bread! It's very squashy in with all the other bits of bread, but someone's got to do it! I'm taken out of the loaf and this sludgy yellow stuff is spread all over me, then this ugly brown stuff they call Marmite is spread on top.

I'm packed into a small box along with an apple, crisps, yoghurt and a chocolate bar. We are stuffed into a bag and taken to some place called school. I'm really not keen on this place!

We're shoved into a locker for the morning, the apple starts to turn brown and the chocolate starts to melt. I am a couple of days old and all these green bits keep popping up all over me.

It's lunchtime now; the box I'm in is taken out of the locker and taken into the dinner hall. Some giant animal-looking thing takes the lid off. At last there is air! The animal takes the apple and chucks it in the bin, the chocolate bar and yoghurt are gobbled down. I'm taken out of the box and placed on the table. This is it! The lid is placed on top of the box and that huge animal thing walks off. I'm left here in the middle of the table with all this brown gloopy stuff coming out of me. I am left in a world where no one likes Marmite! Noooo . . .

Cherryanne Pullinger (14)
Priory Community School, North Somerset

DISAPPEARANCE

Faith waved goodbye to the movers as they drove down the winding drive in the now empty removal van. She loved moving house, she had moved five times since she had left the orphanage. Faith had been restless living in the same place for over 16 years, only going out for day trips once a month, so now she moved every chance she got.

That night she was awoken by a noise. She sat upright, peering into the corner she was sure the noise had come from. Slowly, smoothly, almost gliding a large figure stepped out of the shadows. It was definitely human, cloaked in a long, black hood. It outstretched a hand towards her, cold, clammy giving off an icy vibe. Faith stood up quickly and scrambled to the wall, backing against it.
'Get away!' she screamed. There was no answer. It came closer.
'Get lost, leave me alone!' Sobbing she grabbed at the cross that hung around her neck and held it out in front of her, trying to warn it away.
'Please!' she begged, 'just leave me alone!'
It came closer.
'Please,' she sobbed.
It came closer still.
She slid to the floor as her knees gave way with fear and covered her head with her arms. With one last muffled sob from Faith the hand was laid gently on her shoulder. Then they were gone. Nothing was left, but mis-matched furniture in a small, dark room that had just two seconds ago been filled with sobs and screams.

Neither figure had walked out the door or climbed out the window and shimmied down the drainpipe, or even magically walked through the wall. Both of them just simply . . . *disappeared!*

Jessica Hooper-Gauci (14)
Priory Community School, North Somerset

D-Day Landings, Your Finest Hour

June the 6th 1944, 6am. D-Day landings. The English and American forces were landing on the beaches of Normandy.

The landing crafts landed. The doors came crashing down and out of each craft charged 15 soldiers, to what would probably be their bloody deaths. It was a horrible sight, hundreds of young solders dying . . . lives wasted. As they tried harder and harder to survive, eventually nearly giving up.

But there was one soldier that would never give up, his name was Jack Stewards, a 19-year-old boy forced to join the army, but he had come too far to give up now. He looked brave, but inside he was scared.

Hours passed of non-stop fighting. Only a few soldiers reached the top of the beach, including Jack.

Just then in the sky, out of nowhere, appeared a dark, gloomy thing. It looked like a helicopter, but it was a plane, a Messerschmidt. It flew overhead firing as it went, but only hitting dead people.

A whistling noise drowned out the cries of dying people. It was a bomb. Followed by the whistling was a large explosion, there were more whistling noises as a massive bomb crashed down on a bunker. It was probably a mistake. But it was still hit.

Rocks went flying, crushing a few people. Blood was everywhere including Jack's. The medics tried to save him but he had lost too much blood and died.

Lawrence Rowland (11)
Priory Community School, North Somerset

A Day In The Life Of Doffryn

There he stands triumphant, his axe in tight grip, his enemy slain. This is just another day, another battle for Doffryn the Barbarian.

He is prime defender of the Doffrynites, a large clan in the centre of Coldor (the world he lives in), he dresses in his mithril armour, given to him by his father when he was a boy warrior, his leather boots and skull helmet. He wields his favourite weapon, his steel double-ended axe. He has seen off many a man with this and some other things like elves, goblins and sprites.

He has no fear in his heart, but the fear of his clan being overruled by his most hated enemy, the Thane of Crystalalis. An evil, hate-loving ogre who lives in the mountain of Crystal.

Their hatred towards each other has spanned across Doffryn's life since he was a boy warrior, the age of nine, when the Thane of Crystalalis invaded the village where Doffryn's mother lived while Doffryn was on a quest with his father and killed his mother.

So since then his whole life he has searched for a moment of vengeance for his mother's death. Always searching, never stopping, every day getting one step closer to freeing his mother's soul and his conscience and clearing the world of the evil that dwells within it.

Mark Bell (14)
Priory Community School, North Somerset

THE PROBLEM FAMILY

The problem family, there was a mum who was a blonde-haired woman with blue eyes, wonky nose and a big mouth. Then there was Dad, he had brown hair with brown eyes, a straight nose and small mouth. He also had a goatee. Then there was their kids. The elder one Sam was 13 and the younger one Ben was 10.

They lived in a small house because they didn't have very good jobs. The boys shared a room, it was a *tip*. It looked like a bomb had hit it. There were clothes on the floor, smashed glass, broken cupboards, drawers and beds. I think a bomb had hit it!

Their mum and dad's room, was the biggest room in the house which was still pretty small, had a king-sized bed which took most of the room, they had two small cupboards and that was it.

Now we go downstairs into the living room and guess how big it is? It is the smallest room you have ever seen in your life. It has one, one-seater sofa, and one small and when I say small I mean small, television and a window, that is it.

The last room is the kitchen, it has normal kitchen things, but they are all smaller than usual and that's all about the house. And then there is the garden, but that is a whole new story.

Mitchell Ford (11)
Priory Community School, North Somerset

A Day In The Life Of A School Bag

My owner picks me up. Lunch gets put in me.

Get picked up and put on owner's back and carried out into the cold streets. I hate it when it rains because I only hold so much rain before it starts to seep through. The weight of my contents starts to ache my straps. When I arrive at school I get thrown under a desk on the cold damp floor. I hate the smell of the floor. Why can't they clean it with something that smells nice?

I then get used as a ball. It really hurts and I always get dirty. It's a pain in my straps.

When the teacher comes I sit under the desk for ages. It's so boring. Under the desk is the worst place to be. The dry, crispy chewing gum has been under the desk for most of its life. But the worst thing is when I get used as a footrest. I always get squashed and I hate it.

Break; the thing I hate most. I always get thrown on the cold tennis court floor. I get thrown about and my owner doesn't care! I hate him so much.

Three more lessons left. I hate being a school bag. It's so painful and lonely and when I get home I get thrown in the corner and left. Then the whole cycle starts again. I hate my life!

Matthew Brown (14)
Priory Community School, North Somerset

NIGHTMARE

He was so cold, feet so dead, numb and lifeless like the night itself. He soon arrived outside the castle and went up to knock on the door, but found it slightly ajar. So he stepped inside being conscious of what was around him. The door, carried by the wind, swung shut.

The castle was very dark and had a damp smell inside. As he was walking down the creaky, winding staircase, hanging crookedly on the wall from a rusty old nail was a dusty picture of an old man covered in cobwebs.

He searched around to see if anyone was there that could help him, but he soon came across a huge wooden door with a rusty key hanging on the cracked stone wall next to it. He picked up the key and tried to open the door. He fiddled about with the lock until he found himself stumbling inside.

The room was pitch-black with a rotten stench. He found a broken switch on the wall and pressed it, on came a flickering bulb swinging back and forth from the stained ceiling.

He gasped in horror at the awful sight of about ten dead bodies hanging from nooses, nailed to the huge wooden beams, eaten away by woodworm. There was also one freshly hung noose which made it almost seem as if he was meant to get lost and find his way to the castle and that that fresh noose was for him.

A voice suddenly woke him from his sleep.
'You were having a nightmare.'

Heidi Kyte (14)
Priory Community School, North Somerset

GRANDMA

Friday
It was starting again and it scared me. I knew why it scared me. I knew what it was. Grandma. She would be there, sitting on the battered sofa, crying. Why she cries she never tells. Nobody's dead. She's got a job as a music therapist, so there's enough money for food and stuff, she should be happy.

I walked over to her. She looked up, her pale blue eyes now red and puffy. I told her not to cry, everything was OK. She smiled, unconvincingly and I went to school.

That night in bed I heard it again; loud sobs coming from the living room. I huddled up under the coffee-stained covers, trying to muffle the pitiful sound. I drifted into an uneasy sleep.

Saturday
Morning. Breakfast. Crying. Today I should be out with Naddy. I told myself Grandma will be fine on her own. Naddy shouted, 'Hurry up, your grandma will be fine on her own!'

I believed her - why?

I get home. I put the key in the lock. I wasn't nervous, at that moment I didn't know there was anything to be nervous about. Then I walked in. I could never forget what I was about to see.

An empty pill bottle. Foamy vomit on the carpet and around Grandma's mouth. And Grandma sprawled over the sofa, her eyes were marbles in her snowy skin. I screamed. She was dead.

Lara Stenner (12)
Priory Community School, North Somerset

HALLUCINATION

My head was spinning, I couldn't think. The SATs paper was sitting in front of me, untouched. It was like being in a washing machine, going around and around in circles, always coming back to the same ideas. I looked around the classroom, pens were scribbling, the noise got louder, the walls were closing in on me . . . I stared at the lined paper on the table, it stared back and laughed.

Still, the pens were scribbling away and growing louder. I was locked in a room that was shrinking. The washing machine in my head got faster, yet the paper remained untouched by my blue Biro and even *that* began to laugh.

Sweat ran down my forehead and trickled down my neck, but it didn't bother me. Suddenly the washing machine broke down and I started scribbling stuff onto the paper, it was still laughing, but its throat was hoarse and it soon gave up and went to sleep. My Biro was running across the page, it was panting, but it kept going. Things were eventually returning to normal.

The egg timer sitting on the teacher's desk went berserk and let off a loud buzz, when it fell off the desk, the teacher stood on it. He eyed everybody carefully as we stood up and walked out of the room to break.

Oooh . . . scary!

Kate Evans (11)
Priory Community School, North Somerset

THE MURDER OF ST SLYVESTER WOODS

It was stalking me. There was no doubt about it. I began to run, but it ran too. I could have been shrouded in the crisp autumn leaves, but I was too frightened to think straight. I could hear the rustle of moistureless foliage drawing nearer and the desperate heavy breathing of me, apart from that an eerie silence. The rustle came closer every second that passed.

As I ran further, the woods thickened and barely any daylight passed through the branches. Each tree stood like a giant, frozen in time. I had more to worry about though. A lot more.

If I wanted to get home alive, I had to think fast. I sprang into a nearby bush hoping that it would be a good enough disguise. As I leapt into it though, its branches snapped creating more noise than I had anticipated. I could only run as it got closer to me.

Run, run, run! I couldn't think of anything else. The trees weren't getting easier to see through. Each leaf was like a steel barrier pushing my muscles harder and harder until I felt them give up. As I looked back, still running, I tripped over a tree root from out of the ground like a bear trap, just waiting.

It caught up with me and I felt a horrific pain. Was that my blood or its blood? Without warning everything went pitch-black. That was the last I ever remembered.

Chloe Loader (12)
Priory Community School, North Somerset

NAKATA MAKES IT BIG

It has been announced today that the £13,000,000 midfielder Hidetoshi Nakata has failed to sign a new contract with Parma AC. He was supposed to sign for £50,000 but failed to sign on the deadline. He has been talking to Liverpool for a few months and has signed for five years on a salary of £75,000 per week.

The Japanese international who has been captain for a number of years has left his number ten shirt and said earlier, 'I am glad I've signed for Liverpool and I hope to stay there for the rest of my career.'

Whilst he was at Parma AC he never had a good relationship with his former manager. He was reported to have hit Nakata but denied all charges and was later cleared.

The Liverpool manager, Gerard Houllier has known Nakata for a number of years but has never been able to sign him.

The versatile midfielder showed his skills off at the 2002 World Cup by taking Japan into the final stages.

Nakata will be joining stars such as Michael Owen and Steven Gerrard at Liverpool and will fit perfectly into the centre of midfield or on the wing.

He will be one of the most creative players in the Premiership.

Joshua Redmond (12)
Priory Community School, North Somerset

A Day In The Life Of J R R Tolkien

Dear Diary,

This day I have only 24 hours to live and then I'll die in pain or be put to sleep.

I have a large bank account and write lots of books, like 'Lord Of The Rings'. My brother Chris has been a very good, loyal and helpful brother to me, helping me through my work.

I also have some things to say before I die, and here they are:
I give all my money to my wife and to Chris (half each).
I give my beautiful house to my beautiful wife,
And half of my book money to Chris, the other half to my wife.

No Diary! I will not stay in bed for the rest of my life. I will go outside and tell you what my last day is like.

It's all sunny, unlike me (I'm old and boring with no mind). I wish my life was like this, but it's not, unfortunately. Well I will spend the rest of my day describing the rest of my life.

There are birds singing in the air and there's a slight breeze. Well that's what it's like at the moment, cloudless also. I love it out here and I wish this day would never end and so do I wish my life would never end, but everybody has to die some time and my time has come now.

Goodbye everybody, have a happy ending - because mine ends here!

William Price (12)
Priory Community School, North Somerset

A Day In The Life Of Elvis Presley

Dear Diary,

I am sorry I haven't written in you for ages, but at this time of day I think I'll have to write about what the rest of my life will be like - in you Diary and I'm writing about what future I'll have.

I only have a few weeks to live and I have a few words to say, which is that I hope my family will live their lives better than I did and I wish I could have done a few things better than I did. I can't say what they are because they're personal and I can't even tell you Diary. The other thing is that I wish I could have been a better person to everybody else. Even though I know I am famous and everybody likes me as a singer and a friend.

Now Diary, I must go outside and look around for the last time in my short life. I will come back and tell you all about it.

Well Diary, it was fun and I enjoyed seeing people again because people said hello and asked for my autograph, which made me feel young and happy again inside. Also it made me feel and see the wonders of the world.

So here we are Diary, saying goodbye to each other on this last paragraph. Gooodbye everybody and thank you very much.

                                                          Elvis Presley

Matt Hedges (11)
Priory Community School, North Somerset

THE BROKEN LACE

It was Saturday the 31st of March, John had to wait four long days till the football match. His mum Judy kept on nagging him about the laces for his boots.
'I'm only doing it for you and your team's sake,' said his mum.
John always said he would do it later on!

The next day Judy said, 'If you don't buy some laces you'll have no pocket money for four weeks!'
John bought some laces and went home at the speed of light. When he got home, his mum stood there with unfinished football homework. John's homework was about who was playing and what position they were playing in.

John woke up with a yawn, ran down the stairs and had a slice of toast with Judy still pestering him about the laces. After he finished he went to get the laces. 'Where are they?' he yelled. He would have to do without.

At the game it was going fine at 3-2 to their rivals. One of the players had been fouled *'Penalty!'* John had to take it, if he scored his team would win the cup. His mum and his friends cheered. He ran up just before he hit the ball and the lace snapped and his boot flew off!

Martin Thomas (12)
Priory Community School, North Somerset

BEOWULF, OR NEIGHBOURS FROM HELL

Hwaet - Listen, we have heard of the glory of the Kings of the Danes in ancient days, how those brave princes did great deeds, but what you hear less about is their tuneless singing - at all hours of the night - and barbaric behaviour!

I used to live in a nice quiet, peaceful little swamp, my mum and me (Grendal), but then Hrothgar moved into Heorot next door, along with all his Danish mates. Now, I'm not adverse to a little mead and gentle music once in a while but I draw the line at drunken parties every night of the week, lasting into the early hours.

I hadn't slept in weeks thanks to their trumpet blowing and mead guzzling, so I thought I'd just pop round and ask them politely to turn the harps down and give the mead barrels a rest.

I have never been treated so badly in all my life! As I walked into the room they began hurling insults and reaching for their swords. Believe me if they'd been saying those things about your mother you'd have gone mad too. Perhaps breaking arms off and chewing heads was a bit excessive, but we've all been there, haven't we?

Well after that, every time I've heard their music and drunken laughter I go round to shut them up. It's become a habit.

Cowards! That's what they are, cowards, can't stop me complaining on their own, need their Geat mates to help them. Tonight I guarantee there is going to be one big party. Those Geats don't scare me though. Their party's going to end sooner than they expected . . .

'They've killed him! They've killed Grendal my little lad. He had just enough strength to struggle home to me after they hacked his arm off. I think tomorrow I'll give them a piece of my mind. No bunch of drunken Danes and their Geat mates do that to my little boy and get away with it.'

Hannah Whittock (13)
St Laurence School, Wiltshire

The Art Gallery

The art gallery was black - midnight-black. The walls were disguised by the elegant, luxurious folds of the huge, black tapestries that dangled from the ceiling. The carpet was grey and dusty. The lighting was dimly yellow and subtle. The atmosphere was quiet, but chilly and tense, the smell of air freshener lingering on the edge.

As I walked through the gallery, my movements were followed by dozens of pairs of cold, staring eyes. The ageing pictures, with fading colours, framed with curling gold leaf regarded all with a discreet, emotionless countenance. The subjects had yellowing skin and crumbling paint, but they held a certain presence, an icy feeling.

I took another step forward and another. Suddenly my foot snagged on a loose piece of carpet. I tumbled forward, madly clawing at the thin air for support. I turned my fall into a lunge at the nearest chair. My knee skidded on the floor, burning painfully and I went careering, arms flailing into a piece of screening. There was a horrendous ripping, then a small, innocent *ping* and to my horror one of the ancient pictures came tumbling down with a tremendous clash and clatter.

The place fell silent. A surge of terror flooded my soul. The canvas had torn into two and disintegrated. It lay, crinkling, forlorn on my knees. The shock overwhelmed my face and I flushed crimson. I felt hot. I began to shake and sweat, the world spinning out of focus. Desperately, I swept the remains beneath a display cabinet and strode off, legs wobbling, willing myself, madly, to look normal.

A disturbed, fierce, rustling whisper seemed to hiss out of the paintings. I heard a faint crackle behind me.

I felt a hand on my shoulder. I jumped, my heart somersaulting. The hand was heavy and it was clinging to me with claw-like fingers, almost gouging my flesh. It was warped, fading and crackling.

Swish! Thud! The world was black, midnight-black . . .

Niall Allsopp (13)
St Laurence School, Wiltshire

PVC FUGITIVE

Mr Roberts, with his leaf rake, walked slowly across the courtyard, his face tautly stretched across the grey sky, alight with fiery reds and golds. He was caretaker here; no one should be able to laugh at him. But he saw them, peering out the windows. Boys laughing, girls pretending to be sick. As the headmaster had also said, 'It's difficult to find people who fit the description as well as you'd like. But I'm sure we can make an exception here, applicants are scarce.' And then there'd be the wince as they looked away, every time.

Stuff him. Stuff all those stuck up heads. He's seen them all, from school to school, college to university. All the same. They just wouldn't give him a chance. It was lucky none of it went on his record or he'd never get a job again. Not after his 'assaults'. He didn't like to call them that, he preferred 'paybacks' or 'attitude adjustments'. Well it never would go on *his* record would it? It would go on someone else's, someone he had invented. One year he might be Mr Simmons, another Mr Jones. Easy. His face could be changed to whoever he wanted to be. The police weren't going to catch him.

So his face might be just like everyone else's. Maybe it was a little odd not having any facial expressions or a sideways nose.

But what do you expect from an underpaid plastic surgeon?

Max Mulvany (12)
St Laurence School, Wiltshire

WORST WORLD WAR II

It was my turn to sign up for the war, I felt a tremor all the way down my body, my hair stood on end and my arm shook. I had just entered the Second World War, most probably never to leave it, alive.

We had a few weeks of training which taught the basics of how to fire and reload a gun. We had no idea when we were going to go to the trenches. Then one day we were all squashed into a lorry, the looks on everyone's faces were dull, gloomy and scared.

When we were finally dropped off, we stepped onto a muddy footpath, where we were greeted by an officer, who led us to the trenches. I could hear people crying while looking at their families on pictures.

Explosions and gun shots were being fired non-stop. The puddles were deep, the mud covered my boots and it rained like tomorrow. I found my own spot in the trench and put down my belongings. I made a friend called Sam, he had been here for three days and he didn't talk much, as he constantly shook with fear.

Our commanding officer walked past and said, 'Fifteen minutes lads, you're up.'

The minutes seemed like hours, no one spoke. On the fifteenth minute I collected my pride, jumped over and ran. My men beside me started to fall, then it was my turn, *bang!*
I was dead.

Adam Morgan (14)
Stonyhurst College, Lancashire

THE LOTTERY TICKET

It's just one of those days, Mum is working all the time to get some money, but she is so tired. We are still really short on money. I need some new shoes for school, my old ones have holes in the soles. I never see Dad, he is always at the pub. When he comes home late he is really drunk and they argue.

When we weren't so short of money, once a week, my dad would buy a lottery ticket, but we never really won much, apart from £10. We stopped when we couldn't afford it. It's my birthday next week, I don't expect to get much, all I want is my family around me, which I have.

One day I hope that all our worries will be over and we can go on holiday to Spain. I have decided to get a job at weekends, it will get me out of the house. I am going to go round the neighbours and ask if they want any odd jobs doing. I hope to have made enough money in a weekend to buy a few lottery tickets.

I am sitting with three lottery tickets in my hand, all the numbers were special occasions. The balls had started rolling. One number came out, it was my mum's birthday. Then the rest came up and they were all mine, my *heart* stopped, we had won!

Charlotte Walsh (13)
Stonyhurst College, Lancashire

THE BEGGAR

Every day I walk past the doorway of an old, unused factory on my way to work. Every day I see the same old man sitting in the same old place, wrapped tight in his worn out sleeping bag with his only companion, his dog, lying next to him. His tartan flat cap lies empty on the floor and the look of desperation on his face as he plays his dark blue recorder forces me to toss a pound or two into the cap. He smiles, sometimes even says, 'Thank you,' or 'God bless.'

Sometimes I go into the small café around the corner and walk past the beggar to get to my bus stop. As I walk past I toss the dog part of a bacon sandwich, which he gobbles down as if he were never fed; by the looks of him, I doubt he ever is.

I sometimes see him come out of the newsagents and tear apart a chocolate bar or an apple, or pour a drink down his throat. Every day is a struggle for him, to keep himself alive and his dog. It's people like me, who give him our spare change, that keep him alive.

Gregory Kelly (14)
Stonyhurst College, Lancashire

ANOTHER TERRORIST ATTACK

After what happened on September 11th, 2001 would you believe that another terrorist attack greater than that would happen two years on? Well an attempt was made . . .

On 29th August 2003 the FBI heard of a terrorist organisation named the 'Cobra'. This group had all the equipment they needed to build a nuclear weapon which could destroy the world. However by September nothing more had been heard of them, so the police felt that there were, more urgent matters to deal with. A disturbance however brought them back up to the top of the suspicion list when a phone call was made by the leader of the gang, King Cobra. It warned the President that he should evacuate Washington for a nuclear weapon was going to be dropped on the White House and that it would destroy the whole world.

The President was immediately evacuated, however over the next week nothing happened so the President returned. Yet another call was made and the call was traced to New York City. It offered the police a chance to stop them dropping the bomb if they paid $50,000,000. The President was informed and with the FBI came up with a plan. King Cobra said that he would call in 10 minutes time to see if they wanted to pay up or face the consequences . . . and sure enough he did.

A car drove up outside a coffee shop and dropped 2 suitcases off, filled with the money. A swift change was made and nothing more was heard, however the suitcases were not filled with money but paper so the King Cobra told them that this was their last chance and as he said that a bomb was dropped from the sky. This was no ordinary bomb, it was filled with custard as cold as ice and it fell right on top of the White House. The President was furious, however the terrorist organisation could not be found and the police are still looking for them.

So, be warned, if ever you see a big balloon dropping from the sky move out of the way . . . unless you like custard!

Isabella Gee (13)
Stonyhurst College, Lancashire

CLOSE SHAVE IN AFRICA

We had been chasing the poachers for two days now and I was beginning to lose hope. We had found a dead elephant with a shotgun wound in its side and its tusks gone. My Kalahari companion, Chakanaka, had quickly found the tracks of a truck and we have followed the curvy markings in the sand.

Chakanaka beckoned to me in the light of the African dawn. In the distance, dust was rising. Something out there had started moving, too small to be a herd of buffalo or impala, but just about the right amount for a large vehicle.

We jumped into action. The poachers were not expecting any resistance and so did not travel at too fast a speed. We could easily catch up in our Land Rover.

We overtook the truck and swerved in front of it, causing it to slam on its brakes. Through the dust I could see a solitary figure get slowly out of the truck, hands on his head. Chakanaka had said that there were two sets of footprints; I wondered where the other poacher was. I told Chakanaka to stay in the Land Rover.

As I approached the tall figure, something shone in my eye. I realised that the sun had reflected off a gun barrel, pointing at me! I dived into the undergrowth, then came a gunshot.

Chakanaka was standing by our Land Rover, revolver pointed at the truck. He had shot the poacher, wounding his hand, saving my life! We brought the two poachers back to the authorities and they spent a long time in jail.

Timothy Lewis (14)
Stonyhurst College, Lancashire

A Day In The Life Of . . . A Soldier

Life on the front line isn't much fun. All we see are hours upon hours of bombing and after that, men upon men dying, but the thing that counts is that we are defending Britain from Hitler and the Nazis.

I wish one day this war would end so I can get back and carry on with my life. Have a family and become a grandad and be able to tell stories of how hundreds of thousands of men died trying to keep England English.

Today I think we are going to have a push again and I expect that I will die and I hope I am remembered by someone at home. Life on the front line is hard because if you make any friends, they will be dead the next day.

I've only got five minutes until we go over and the nerves are starting to kick in. I see death in the men all around me, all I hope is that they're not covering my back when my time comes.

I've just heard the whistle, we're going. I look side to side and men are falling all over the place. I take cover on a bomb hole, then I see my captain duck so I run over to find one of his legs is missing. I pick him up and carry him back, then I feel a pain in my chest, I've been shot . . .

Anthony Hines (14)
Stonyhurst College, Lancashire

A Day In The Life Of An Unemployed Man

As the wife drew the curtains back, the sunrays hit me like a stone smashing glass. As I found my bearings, the aching pounded my head. The stale smell of crushed beer cans and the stench of smoke fumes filled the room. I looked up at the four walls surrounding me which were spinning like a merry-go-round. I said to myself, *another day, drinking beer and looking for a job.* 47 years old and still unemployed, where have all those years gone?

I managed to drag myself across the room to have a look at the clock, 12.20, it read. I had to force myself upstairs and put a shirt on and find a new pair of trousers because the other pair were marked with a stain of cigarette ash. I pulled myself downstairs and threw the door open. I stepped out onto the littered pavement and crossed the road into the Job Centre.

After a long time searching as usual, no jobs with good pay for little work. Half an hour of clicking a mouse only to find bitter disappointment and I felt bad enough so crossed the road like it was a walk of shame and went into my house. For the rest of the day I sipped beer after beer until I fell asleep with the same walls spinning round and round and round.

Robert Plumbridge (14)
Stonyhurst College, Lancashire

THE SOLDIER

The soldier lay tense and still under the towering trees soaring high into the sky. Bugs and creepy-crawlies scurried around looking for victims to scorn, kill and carry back to base camp. It is amazing how two totally different beings can have the same objective. Yet the soldier was alone in solitude, more agitated and nervous of the events, which had not yet come to pass.

He thought of happy times with his wife and children, when they would all play in the back garden with the sun beating with intense heat. Then he glanced at himself and his surroundings. He was a lonely child, lost in the dark, with no one to turn to.

The pitter-patter of rain on the mud, his uniform and gun were like endless echoes ringing in his ears from a very far distance.

All fell silent . . . nothing was to be heard anywhere. The soldier looked around in disarray at his comrades. There was an atmosphere of panic and rush as he fumbled for his rifle. A short yet sharp pain down his right leg, he bellowed and screamed for help, but it seemed that his mouth opened and only air was let out. He looked around again and realised that what he had been waiting for, in the cold and wet for five days and nights alone, was now taking place. Despite all the warnings, he felt the event dormant and non-existent.

A friend ran over and whispered, 'We are unimportant.' He fell limply over the soldier and he slowly fell asleep with tears running down his cold, pale, stone face.

Dane Cimpoias (14)
Stonyhurst College, Lancashire

You Never Know

You never know why or what is watching you. When you walk through a forest, or even down a road, there could be someone or something watching you. You never know what is happening around the corner, or behind a closed door, right next to you.

It is really quite a scary thought when you think about it. I feel extremely left out when I realise what I am missing out on. Even in the same house secrets will be kept from you and me.

Walking to school in the morning, a secret admirer may be staring at you, or there may be an enemy watching you with hatred in his eyes. All of the time, we are totally oblivious to this.

No one and nothing like not knowing but when you do know, you wish you didn't but only if it is bad. If you find out something that gives you hope, or peace, or maybe even joy, then knowing is a great thing.

This is always a gamble when the question *what?* is asked. It's like a game, if you are lucky then knowing is great, but if you are unlucky then you cannot turn back on anger.

This is a vicious circle of future when you don't know, you want to know, and when you know, you wish you had never asked. The moral of the story is *you never know!*

Gregory Wood
Stonyhurst College, Lancashire

MY LAST CHANCE

Rob Keneval was an upcoming star in the world of the stuntman, he was young and had everything going for him but when he and his Kawasaki motorbike got into some trouble in the middle of a daredevil stunt there were big decisions to make.

Rob ended up in the sunny city of Santa Cruz but it wasn't for a vacation. He was in the world's best bone-building clinic, where he was told hesitantly that he would no longer be able to be a stuntman. It wasn't that easy, the buzz Rob got from the adrenaline was what kept him alive.

After four weeks of bone-building and inserting metal rods into his back, Rob was up and strolling around. The doctors were saying that Rob was ready to leave, but the only thing holding up his back was the steel spike, so he still would not be able to ride.

When Rob came out of the hospital he was met by his flashy producer, Damien Sharks, who told him of a stunt which would make him enough money to settle down for life. Rob thought of the consequences but took the job.

Damien did not hesitate and rushed off with Rob to the jump site which was a great canyon.

Rob made the jump but on landing, jolted his spine which resulted in two years in a wheelchair. Rob donated half his money to creating a charity which helped stuntmen who had been in crashes getting back to full health.

Robert Woolley (14)
Stonyhurst College, Lancashire

THE LAST CHANCE

It seemed an ordinary day, no different to any other. I woke up in the morning, came downstairs for a glass of milk and they were there, just staring at me as if I'd done something wrong. I was quite worried, what had happened? Had someone died? I was thankful that I was looking straight at both Mum and Dad because Dad had been ill for quite some time and Mum had fallen ill a couple of months ago, so I knew they were alright.

'Mum, Dad why are you looking at me as if I'll never see you again? You do realise I love you both, don't you?' I walked promptly into the kitchen, looked around and there they were. They looked familiar . . . they were the same two men that had brought me to my mum and dad. You see Mum and Dad aren't my blood parents but my foster parents.

'What's wrong? What's happened?' I went and sat down in-between Mum and Dad.
They both put their arms around me and said, 'Rachel you do realise we love you and nothing can take that away from us, but because we're both so ill and you only being ten years old, can't look after yourself, we are going to have to give you to some other parents that will look after you even better than we have and are younger and fitter and will be able to play games in the garden and have fun with you. We will have to say goodbye this afternoon. We know it's very sudden and you have been a pleasure to live with, but this afternoon will be the last chance to say goodbye to all your friends and say goodbye to us. We hope you won't go far so if you could occasionally visit us, that would be wonderful.'

Yvette Spedding (13)
Stonyhurst College, Lancashire

QUESTIONING THE SPOOKS

It had just turned dusk and Laura was standing in the freezing driveway in the moonlight, saying goodbye to her husband, who was off to work his nightshift at the local printing factory.

The newlyweds had only just moved into their new home. It was bigger and brighter than their last council house, Laura stepped into the half-decorated hallway and sighed, then walked into the living room and collapsed heavily between the many unpacked boxes onto the sofa, which she had inherited from her grandmother. They had just returned from their honeymoon a week before and everything was still in a mess.

As she sat down on the sofa, the ten o'clock news suddenly came onto the TV, Laura froze, then when she realised that she had sat on the remote, she relaxed again.

She had had reason before now to suspect that the newly converted barn was haunted. The first night they had spent there, they had heard strange noises from the dining room, a noise, like boxes being moved around, but there was no one else in the house. She didn't let it bother her after all, no one else had complained of spooky goings on, so she was probably worrying about nothing. Well she didn't worry until: *knock, knock.*

She felt a breath catch in her chest, her heart was pounding. She had heard no one come up the path. Then again, *knock, knock.* Then the letter box flapped open, 'Love, I've forgotten my keys.' It was her husband.

Annabel Gale (14)
Stonyhurst College, Lancashire

AND IT GREW COLDER...

The evening sky was totally clear, a deep midnight-blue. Even the most distant star could be seen and it was cold. Already, early in the evening, rime had settled on the grass and was spreading over gates and fences. It was so still not a leaf stirred on the deserted sidewalk.

As the glacial night wore on, the stars disappeared behind an advancing blanket of dark cloud. The temperature rose slightly as large snowflakes began to settle, falling like fuzzy, white polka dots and drifting silently to the ground. No one stirred and the temperature plummeted.

One man awoke in the early hours, shivering uncontrollably. Still half-asleep, he stared around his room and realised the reason for his incipient hypothermia; the window was open, and a substantial drift was forming on the nearby area of carpet. Blearily, he shoved the window closed, vaguely hoping that he wouldn't have a flood on the floor later. He needn't have worried, the ambient temperature in his room was already below zero and wasn't about to rise again.

The early morning advanced steadily into daytime. Gradually, the wintry village came to life. Sleepy eyes opened to a strange grey dawn that was too bright for moonlight and too dull for the sun. Children squealed in delight and rushed for their sledges, while parents struggled with taps that wouldn't work.

The entire world seemed gripped in a frigid vice of intense cold, as unrelenting as it was beautiful.

Anne Rawsthorn (14)
Stonyhurst College, Lancashire

THE UNWELCOME ARRANGEMENT

As a member of a family that was highly dedicated to the Muslim faith, Meera's destiny was to be married to a complete stranger of her parents' choice. She had no choice in the matter and was distraught when she met her future husband. It was clear from the beginning that the two were not going to get along and she immediately began to think of ways of escaping from what she thought would turn out to be a living hell.

Meera felt that she desperately needed something to take her mind off the whole situation. She rang her best friend Laura, who suggested that a night of partying would do the trick.

After having travelled in an overly crowded taxi, Meera was at the entrance of the club in the middle of a huge crowd of strangers. She followed them into a huge hall, which was swarming with people. She could hardly hear herself think and the flashing lights around her made her head spin uncontrollably. Before she could pull away, a hand grabbed her by the arm and dragged her towards the bar. Within seconds, a glass was thrust into her hand and she felt a cold thrill as the tangy taste hit her like a bullet. After several more drinks, she found she was no longer in control of her body and the next thing she remembered was waking up in a strange bed in a room she did not recognise. As she sat up in the bed, a dark man entered the room and smiled at her. After a terrifying second, she realised who he was. It was her fiancé, Neeraj . . .

Serena Marchetta (15)
Stonyhurst College, Lancashire

MOVED

The wind blew fiercely in her face. She kept on running. Scared, she looked behind. She tried to penetrate the black shadows. She caught a glimpse of her pursuer, a hooded thug. Drenched in black, he lunged forward. She screamed, a long piercing scream. Desperate, she ran. Thoughts, questions flooded through her mind. Who was he? Why was he chasing her? What would happen to her? Where was she?

After a few hours she slowly dropped, he seemed to have left her and she no longer could fight that throbbing in her leg. Where was she? A rat darted across the damp, broken concrete. She stared at the wall in front of her, it was covered in a thick layer of grime and an open sewer flooded the whole of the narrow alley. It seemed not to affect her though, nothing could. She wondered if she could move?

Slowly she drifted off. She could not quite fall asleep though, shadows were moving, constantly moving, but there was something behind, wandering, whispering. Then it came for her. He dived forward, his hood came off, his dripping dagger sank into her skin, but she never moved. She never moved. She never moved.

Harry Reid (14)
Stonyhurst College, Lancashire

A Wish For The Soldiers

The news is on the TV. Horrible images of war, dereliction and death. For weeks the men in suits have been railing about weapons of mass destruction. People are demonstrating in the streets against the war but it all seems so distant; life goes on.

Yorik my little dog is beside me begging for scraps from my plate. I scratch the wiry brown hair on his back. His sturdy body squirms with excitement as he spies his lead hanging on the door. We set off for our morning walk.

The park is beautiful in the springtime. The wide expanse of green, undulating ground with droplets of dew still hovering above it like a thin silver veil. Gnarled old oak trees bursting with life, what stories they would tell if they could speak. The daffodils are bobbing in the breeze, their golden faces iridescent in the early morning sunlight. All is quiet.

The stillness is suddenly shattered by two raucous blackbirds striding out of the hedgerow, squabbling and flying at each other in a territorial rage. I am reminded of the soldiers fighting, choking with sand, or lying dead in blood and dirt. Then I am choking, with a lump in my throat and heaviness in my chest. Hot tears welling in my eyes for the soldiers and the innocents who have died. The overwhelming futility strikes like a bludgeon on my burning brain. All around me is peace and tranquillity. They should be here. I wish they were here.

Victoria Robinson (15)
Stonyhurst College, Lancashire

Tybra's Journey

I gazed out onto the golden sand dunes, which were reflecting the last bronze rays of the setting sun. The warm soft breeze played with my hair, gently stroking my cheeks. I stood in a daze watching the musky horizon, which reminded me of the glowing charcoal fire in the mud hut I grew up in.

Our hut was small. I felt safe. It was a part of me. Until the day my father told me that I was betrothed to the great warrior Zahi. My heart missed a beat. I was to be married in less than 7 days! Even though I did not want to. I had to escape sooner rather than later. The night welcomed me as I set off with my few possessions. I had left my life behind as I travelled across the barren land.

Days passed, I had lost all sense of time. The desert sun warmed the forever changing variety of sand. At times it seemed endless. During night the air was cold, I often curled up in a ball wishing the impossible.

One day, in the distance, I saw little black specks coming closer. Finding no shelter I began to panic. I was helpless. As the caravan approached, I realised that they were Nomads. Knowing this, however, comforted me a little.

They stopped, moments passed, I marvelled at their elegance. The indigo colour of their cloaks was vibrant against the desert sands. Their clothes were tinted with pale colours, which wove their way through their caftans.

I found refuge in them. It felt like I had never known another life. Years went by and I married. We travelled everywhere together. I felt loved and one of them, Sand, became a faithful travelling companion.

Suddenly I woke up from my daze, my senses returning as I looked up to the velvet sky, millions of stars dancing just beyond my reach. I smiled and thought: *I was no more the girl with nothing, but a woman who couldn't have wished for a happier life.*

Eliza-Maria Warrilow (15)
Stonyhurst College, Lancashire

THAT GLORIOUS DAY

She sat, her legs crossed, upon the soft flesh of the toadstool with her dainty hands folded into each other. Behind her the sun scorched her back and glistened through her delicate cobweb wings. Her face was smooth with an ashen complexion and her chestnut eyes twinkled whilst her long dark hair fluttered in the breeze. Her heart was no longer an empty stone tomb but a warm homely dwelling overflowing with the deepest love and happiness.

He was a prince, his skin was tanned and his auburn hair flopped and waved whilst riding on the backs of dancing butterflies amongst the daffodils and crocuses on a damp spring morning.

It was a perfect day; spring has arrived. The grass was a lush green and the humid air clung to each breath she took. The birds sang harmoniously and the crickets were bounding through the meadows. A nearby pond sparkled in the sunlight and the golden fish basked on the top of the water. She wondered curiously what he would be doing now, she smiled to herself, sank back into her toadstool and closed her eyes.

Kendall Ellen Sharples (14)
Stonyhurst College, Lancashire

THE SNOWFALL

The snow continued to fall into the empty street. Large fluffy flakes fell slowly towards the Earth. They kissed the ground and settled, forming a thick, even blanket over the frozen pavement beneath. A car drove past, the driver wary of the treacherous conditions and disappeared into the curtain of falling snow.

In the gardens of the houses on the street the snow looked crisper, deeper and softer than on the pavement. Children peered out of the front windows of the houses, eagerly awaiting the time when they would be able to go outside to play in the snow. They imagined all the games they could play: snowball fighting or sledging down the nearest hill. The snow continued to fall, whiter than the purest of doves, more graceful than a thousand ballerinas.

A lone man and his dog walked up the street. Their breath condensed in the air as they breathed out, the man's throat stung when he breathed back in, so intense was the cold. His dog whimpered unhappily and nuzzled his owner, wishing deeply to return back to the fireside with a juicy bone. His master, however, was unsympathetic to his pet's needs and continued to trudge through the heavy snow until he too was hidden in the white drape of snow.

Eventually, the snow began to peter out. It fell more slowly, seemingly choosing where to fall. The clouds appeared less dense and some sun shone through them. The snow glittered enticingly and the children finally had their opportunity to enjoy all the fun they could from the snow. Parents were begged into submission and children, wrapped up in hats, gloves and other warm clothes, poured out into the street which was filled with life once again.

James Rawstron (14)
Stonyhurst College, Lancashire

OVER THE TOP

The horrific echoes of the bombs being dropped vibrated in every inch of our trench. We were waiting anxiously for the signal to go over the top. Even though we thought we were not getting anywhere our General told us that we were gaining good ground on the Germans.

I do not know how but I must have drifted into a deep slumber from pure exhaustion, but was abruptly awoken by my closest friend, Billy.
'John, John wake up quick,' he said.

We had orders to get in our positions ready for the dreaded signal.
'Go, go, go!' yelled the General. Everyone clambered out of the mud-ridden, rat-infested trenches and advanced towards the enemy's front line. All around me my fellow soldiers were shot down. The artillery fire was heavy and the noise was defining.
'Back, back, now!' The General wanted us to retreat, things had not gone to plan.

When I got back I scrambled around looking for Billy. 'Billy, Billy, where are you?' I called for him but I knew he had not made it back.
In sheer desperation I threw my weapon down and proceeded to climb over the top.

'Wait, what are you doing?' questioned the General. I explained that Billy hadn't come back and I had to get him.
'Leave him he'll be a gonna!' said the General. Regardless of the General's advice I went over the top. Eventually after falling over many bodies I found Billy. I shook him and called his name, he rolled over, with blood pouring from his chest, he gasped, 'John I knew you'd come,' he clenched my hand and died in my arms.

I carried his limp body back to the trench. When I got there the General said, 'I told you he was a gonna and now you're injured. It was a wasted journey for you.'
I answered him, 'Yes sir I know but all my efforts were worth it, just to hear his last words!'

Natalie Russell-Blackburn (15)
Stonyhurst College, Lancashire

CURIOSITY

This is the story of a happy little monkey. For the purposes of this story we will call him Cosmo. Now Cosmo was a placid, sweet monkey who loved to spend his days swinging in the trees. He lived a carefree life with nothing ever bothering him. He was quite content to play with snakes, or any other jungle creature he found.

One day, Cosmo woke up and there was an odd feeling to the jungle. It was eerily quiet. Cosmo was worried. This sensation was new and unknown to him. He caught a strange scent on the wind. He began to cry out for his friends, but no answer came, he felt so alone. The air became thicker with the new scent, so thick that he couldn't see. He began to cough and splutter. Then he felt it. That horrible prickly heat that set his heart alight.

He ran. All that his monkey brain told him to do was to get away and hide, but there was a strange desire in him that arose. He longed to see what roared with such ferocity. So with this thought dominating his mind he turned. Cosmo wandered slowly through the jungle, with the odd smell burning his throat. When at last he saw the vast expanse of flame in front of him all he could do was stare. Cosmo died an excruciating and painful death.

Ralph Parish (14)
Stonyhurst College, Lancashire

GHOST

Suddenly I was transported to the canopy again. I felt the frosty winter chill surround me. The air was as sharp as nails, to causing little prickles to slide down my throat when I breathed. My fingers were numb and lifeless, and my knees felt like oranges because of the bitter cold. The trees harmonised with the gentle breeze while weightless raindrops silently parachuted from the pale peach sky, one after another. I didn't know exactly where I was; nevertheless my instincts told me that there was light at the end of this hole and that I could find my way out of it. I was yet to find out I was terribly mistaken.

I opened my mouth to scream but no sound came out. To this day I can remember those sadistic eyes from the little girl, and the sinister grin from the dismantled teddy bear she perched under her arm. Her deformed face was a hopelessly grotesque sight; bombarded with bumps and bruises that tore her skin therefore revealing a menacing display of internal tissue. The little girl's sunken eyes stared at me so statically as if they were seeking for the inner core of my soul.

However, the most disturbing factor of the possessed girl wasn't her skeletal and disfigured body shape, nor was it the diseased impression she adopted. But the distressing moaning, endlessly expressed by her, like a thousand daggers drilling into your breast unmercifully. Over and over and over again.

Mwewa Kaluba (13)
Stonyhurst College, Lancashire

ALONE

The best time of the day is at the end of the day. I get in from school at around four. As I open the dark blue door of my house, I quickly slam it shut. I slam away the bad things of the day. Everything is dim and tranquil in the house as Mum and Dad are still at work and won't be home for a few more hours. I like it this way, just me - home alone. I switch on the light in the living room and the familiar surroundings come to life.

After I have got changed out of my school uniform and into my scruffs, I return to the living room. I switch on the TV and some dumb kiddies' programme, the Teletubbies I think, is blaring out at me, but I don't listen, I think. I think about what has occurred during the day, good or bad, but in my case usually bad. This might sound pathetic and stupid but I love being alone. Of course I have mates but they don't understand me properly. No one does! They don't understand my feelings and what I like and don't like. To them I'm just there to talk to when they are upset or hurt but no one offers that to me. I'm just alone.

Lizzie Coles (14)
Stonyhurst College, Lancashire

A Day In The Life Of Tom

Hi I'm Tom, you may get the idea I'm a normal guy with a normal name, a normal dog and a normal life. In fact I am normal, apart from the small fact I haven't got a house.

I've been living on the streets ever since me and Dad had that argument. That was four years ago, god, if I could go back in time I'd never argue again; oops sorry didn't mean to reminisce. Well this time me and Dad didn't sort it out, so I left.

But that's all behind me now, I'm independent, self-reliant, free and have friends, well one friend: Snuffy my dog. Snuffy's a lively, bouncy Yorkshire terrier and he's the only thing that stops me crawling to one of those disgusting shelters; no, really, they don't allow animals, he gives me a reason to live.

I'm quite well known around my area. The reason for this is that I'm sort of well off. You might scoff at that sentence: a well off hobo, there's no such thing. But I am. I earn around £17 per week but I only keep £5 for myself. The rest I give out. Unlike most, the bulk of my money comes from jobs not from kind passers-by.

Every day I get up just before the streets get too busy and go check up on the rest of the homeless in my area and say hello. Then it's off to the shelter where Toni the cook gives me a big box of food rations on one of those two-wheeled trolleys. I then go around Heathrow and give out the food.

After my rounds I go round to the centre and collect my 'Big Issues' so I can sell them on the corner of Chorlston Street till the clock strikes seven. Then it's back to the park for the night.

I sincerely hope I have managed to enlighten you to the fact that the homeless are normal everyday people, not good-for-nothing layabouts.

Mark Ashworth (13)
Wentworth High School, Manchester

THE NOT-SO-ANCIENT MYTH OF MONKEY MAN!

Myths. Myths are ancient beings or old stories told, such as dragons, unicorns and Viking myths, mainly just untrue beliefs, but this one is beyond any of those above, for it is not so ancient. Why, I'm only 13 and I've encountered it. Though, if you ever awake its deep sleep then please be more careful than I was. What I'm trying to say is run and don't stop! For this is the one and only monkey man! OK so it doesn't sound so scary but the saying goes, 'Never judge a book by its cover.' So listen up.

I was walking my dog in the woods behind my house. Buddy strayed ahead, so I started calling his name, 'Buddy, Buddy, come on boy.' I heard a faint growl, so I thought, *yes! He's coming back.* But it wasn't Buddy who returned. It was a big brown monkey at least 30 feet tall with gleaming red eyes and sharp claws. Naturally I ran, as did the chimp, with every step of the monkey's feet came a massive bang. 10 of the longest minutes ever I was pursued by the big ape, then the banging stopped so did I.

I fell to the floor, I opened my eyes and guess what I saw? Yep, you've got it. 'Monkey man!' I screamed.
It picked me up, I shut my eyes and for a weird reason heard a gunshot, another and another. Monkey man fell, as did I (obviously!) I landed with a thud, looked up and saw a tall dark-haired man holding a gun.

He told me the beast was a new species and I encountered it first. I said at the start of this myths were untrue and believe what you want, I know the truth.

Damon Whitbread (13)
Wentworth High School, Manchester

A Day In The Life Of A Tramp

One cold, wet and windy day I was walking down a cobbled street. I saw a tramp; he was wearing ragged clothes. He was full of dust and dirt and he also looked very weary. I sniggered at him.

About five minutes later I arrived home. I started to think about the tramp and started to feel guilty. I started to wonder what he felt and how he dealt with people giving nasty looks, making nasty comments and laughing at him. I went to bed about half ten. I fell straight to sleep.

I woke up the next day. I looked around and I was laying on a cobble street with an old sack for a blanket. I stepped out of the sack and I was wearing old ragged pants and jumper and withered trainers. I looked up at the town clock and it was half eleven on Saturday.

I started to walk around and people sniggered and whispered. I saw my mum and went to talk to her, but she gave me a dirty look. I started to feel alone and scared. Then I saw the tramp, but he was rich. He pointed at me and sniggered. During the day people threw food at me. I ate it because I was hungry and people laughed. At about nine I lay down on the cobbles and went to sleep.

The next morning I woke up in my own bed. I wondered if it was a dream or real?

Sarah-Louise Morris (13)
Wentworth High School, Manchester

THE BIGGEST STORY EVER!

Top reporter for the Daily Alphabet, Lorna Davison, was heading to work on a sunny Tuesday morning at 7.30am. She had caught a cab from her East London flat just 10 minutes ago and was now heading up the street to the head news office on Sycamore Road.

Lorna arrived in the office as usual at 7.35am and sat at her desk waiting for her boss (James Lakington) to give out everyone's assignments for the day. As she waited she looked out over sun-filled Londis Road while drinking a cup of coffee.

Lorna had got her assignment. She was going to Japan to cover the story of a very important ambassador who had just died while giving a public speech (after an apparent heart attack).

The next thing Lorna knew she was in Japan where the culture was very different to East London and the first thing Lorna had to do was change her clothes to fit in. This is because the Japanese did not want reporters hanging around at a time of national mourning. After a day of looking for stories and staying undercover, Lorna retired to her small hotel room and ordered a 6am wake up call.

Three . . . four . . . five or maybe even six wake up calls rang out in Lorna's room but there were no replies, so worried hotel staff went up to see what was wrong and they were met by a horrific sight. Lorna had been stabbed and beaten.

So Lorna finally got her front page story, but for the worst sort of reason.

Victoria Harrison (12)
Wentworth High School, Manchester

The Unmanned Crutches

How boring, isolation, nothing to do, nowhere to go, just paper and a pen on a small one meter square table in front of you. The school couldn't even afford a window just an old PE store room. In fact it was quite spooky!

I looked around, near the door was a blackboard which looked to have been used, the unmanned crutches were for if anybody hurt their ankle or leg in PE. The legend goes that when a boy went in there with a broken ankle, he got locked in there for the summer holidays and when they realised where he was they went to the store room and found only the crutches the boy had used.

Thinking about this made me more and more edgy, every sound made me turn around sharply or even fall off my chair. I stood up and walked over to the corner keeping aware of my surroundings. I took off my sweater and laid it down in the corner and then sat on it. Here I could be aware of everything around me. I felt in my pocket and pulled out a Jolly Rancher. I took it out and popped it in my mouth. Eventually I went to sleep.

I woke up to the clank of metal against concrete. I jumped up almost choking on my sweet. I looked for the crutches, they had moved. My heart beat like a wooden spoon against a frying pan. I ran to the door, it was locked. I looked around. There was a boy looking me in the eyes. I turned around to bang on the door but nobody came. I turned back, the boy was gone.

Robert Grubisic (12)
Wentworth High School, Manchester

HOLD THE FRONT PAGE!

'Why is there never anything good on the front page?' moaned Libby. 'One day we'll make it!' she laughed.
'Oh yeah! doing what!' replied Sophie sarcastically, with a smug grin on her face.
'Rock climbing stupid, just picture it, we'll be on the front page. The best rock climbers in the world.' Joked Libby, posing for her picture that she thought one day would be on the front cover of *all* newspapers!

The girls quickly ran out of the house, as they had just remembered that they were going to High Peak at 10 o'clock, to go climbing.

It was a beautiful day at High Peak. The sun was shining and just a small breeze whispered silently through the trees. The perfect day for rock climbing.

The girls hastily unpacked their bags taking out their lunches, masses of green and purple rope (that looked like a coiled snake), a harness, helmet, first-aid pack, waterproof pants and jacket (even though they didn't need waterproof clothing, the sun was glowing red-hot!), a huge flask of Sophie's favourite drink, orange juice!

The girls, raring to go, ate their lunches quickly. That consisted of jam sandwiches, cheese and onion crisps, an apple, a biscuit and some sherbet lemon sweets. They then walked up the side of the cliff, which wasn't steep, then wrapped their snake ropes around the poles that were already in the ground.

The girls were very excited and as they were running down, Libby tripped over the pole that was smothered in snake rope.
'Argh!' screamed Libby. 'Ow! That hurt, Sophie. I've just banged my leg on that stupid pole, ow, ow, ow!'
'Come on, stupid,' replied Sophie. Sophie jumped and ran off down the blunt edge of the cliff, while Libby hobbled down.

When the girls got to the bottom they hooked up their harnesses to the snake rope and set off up the cliff.
'First one to the top,' shouted Sophie.
'Hang on,' laughed Libby.

Soon the girls were halfway up, but at a very high height!
'Sophie,' shouted Libby in a jerky voice, 'my, my rope, the pole, the pole, it's not right, it's moving, aaargh!'

It was too late, Libby was lying motionless on the floor, only the wind disturbing her beautiful, long golden hair.

Sophie quickly abseiled down and rang for an ambulance. On the way to the hospital, Sophie was nearly as quiet as Libby. Apart from she wasn't on a stretcher and linked up to madly bleeping machines with an oxygen mask on her face.

Luckily Libby was OK and only suffered a broken leg and wrist.

They made it onto the front page of most papers, yes it was to do with climbing! But the picture taken still had Libby doing her same pose that she was doing at home, hugging her best friend Sophie.

Georgina Burrows (12)
Wentworth High School, Manchester

A Day In The Life Of Judy

Judy had lived there all her life; down by the sea where the sand was golden and the sea so blue, but one day wasn't the same as all the rest.

It began just an ordinary day for Judy, a walk down the coastline, a dip in the rock pool, a walk along the sand until . . .

She noticed something, something gleaming in the distance. *What could it be?* she thought to herself. She rushed over full of excitement, *what could it be?* she thought again.

She picked it up. It was a shiny shell, a pearly sandy colour but there was something peculiar about it. She walked towards the sea and dipped it in, it turned blue. At first she was amazed but suddenly she had an idea.

She found a red crab and held the shell near it. It turned red. Now she knew it was a special colour-changing shell, it was magical.

She kept the shell in her room and camouflaged it into her bedroom curtains so that no one could find it.

Three weeks later her mum came in to hoover her room. She took the curtains down and the shell fell onto the carpet.
'Oh no,' cried Judy.
Her mum picked it up. 'What's this?' she asked.
Judy had no answer.

Kathryn Vickers (13)
Wentworth High School, Manchester

A Day In The Life Of A Famous Model!

Living a day in the life of a famous model would seem quite strange and hard.

I woke up early one morning knowing it was going to be different to any other day. Today I was going to live a day in the life of a famous model. I woke up that morning very early having to rush, knowing that I had to be in the studio as early as possible for a dress rehearsal.

When I arrived at the studio I had to be measured because I was a lot bigger than most of the other models. I went looking around the changing room. Looking at all the clothes and the sizes, I thought a size 10 was small but most of the people that wore these clothes were in size 6-8.

Now it was fitting time and I was getting really nervous thinking that I would be walking down with people that were almost anorexic but still looked good. I tried the clothes on, they looked really good and fitted well.

While I was waiting to go up I started talking to one girl called Jadine. She was really nice and said she had done this loads before and still got nervous. That really cheered me up, knowing that I was not the only one. I told her that and it cheered her up as well.

It came to my turn and Jadine's name got called out as well. We realised that we were going up together. Jadine wasn't that much smaller than me so I didn't feel that bad.

I walked up the stage feeling a rush of excitement going through me and then realised I'd loved the day I'd had, but unfortunately it was over and I was wishing that it had never ended.

Sarah Morris (13)
Wentworth High School, Manchester

LEGEND OF LIAM...

Liam, born in 1960 at a very rundown hospital indeed, was recognised as poor to a lot of other civilians living in the area, considering he was restricted to small rations of food, drink and money.

When Liam grew and became a mature teenager he knew he needed to help his family rise above what they had in life. His family and friends loved and respected him and he became popular with the ladies!

Liam got a job later in life at a mechanical factory in Southern Lancashire which he really enjoyed. He took pride in putting on his checked shirt, his ragged pants and hat. His job was to fix the broken machines when they got clogged up or caught. He also supervised new workers.

One night, feeling lonely in the smelly mist of the factory, Liam worked late to gain some money. He had such a hard day the last couple of days and thought he should just rest a bit.

Clog, clob, lob, gob, the machine, the background sounds scared Liam. He thought he should have a look. He jumped under the machine. 'Aarrgghh!' Liam screamed at the top of his voice. He thought he would die, double-taking his last movements maybe of his life, Jimmy came racing round the puddle of blood that was left on the floor.

Where was Liam? What was the matter with him? Had he been sucked away?

Jimmy pulled out a wet cloth and started to mop up the blood that was left still listening for Liam. He squeezed the drops of blood into the bucket. When he heard a chilling laugh in the background.
'Ha, ha, ha, ha!' Liam popped his body round the corner with the head in his hands. 'It's time to die!' he screamed at him.

Liam Bell (12)
Wentworth High School, Manchester

LEGEND OF THE MISSING BALLS

PE, my favourite lesson, time to get away from tedious teachers and tiresome work. It was my turn to get the footballs from the store room. What harm could come from that?

I walked down the corridor which was lined with art by Yr 7. On the left was our trophy cabinet, empty as usual! A cobweb dangled from one corner to the next. On the right was our piano, which people have claimed to hear playing when the school is empty. The store room is at the top of the school along with the attic.

I made my way up the dark, dreary stairs which creaked every three steps. It was enough to make a boxer twitch.

The door was an old oak door with a dusty old number that red 669. Oh wait a minute a number was upside down. It really read 666! Nothing wrong with that. I opened the door slowly. For some reason my heartbeat kept getting faster and faster and then it stopped. I was in the store room, but it was empty.

Later I was in the principal's office sitting on a sort of chair. Mr Porrah walked in with a pipe clanging from his mouth.
'So no ball eh?' questioned Mr Porrah.
'Sir, I didn't nick them.'
'I know.'
'But Sir . . . what . . . ?'
'Ever since the school was built balls have been going missing but we don't know why.'
This confused me but made my mind up about one thing. I was going to find out why balls were going missing!

Max Leonard (12)
Wentworth High School, Manchester